Dearest Dave.
Live Long &
Prosper...
Best Wishes,
G.y.

Dear Dave
well done for
all your hard
work over the
years Lots of love
Em x x

With best wishes
Rob LFB

Britain's Railways in the Second World War

Best
wishes

Bill

Dear Dave,

A Great Big Thank You

from all of us in RIFA,

for all your hard work and

dedication.

Wishing you all the very best

for the future. We will miss you....

Nicole x

BEST WISHES
ANDREW
BROWN

May all your Journey's
be 'Safe'
Take care
Mick Barnes.

HAVE A LONG AND
HAPPY RETIREMENT
DAVID SLAUGHTON

T.C.

14 July 2022

Also by Michael Foley

Britain's Railway Disasters: Fatal Accidents from the 1830s to the Present Day (Pen and Sword, 2019 & 2013)

Essex: Ready for Anything (Sutton Publishing, 2006)

Britain's Railways in the Second World War

Michael Foley

PEN & SWORD
TRANSPORT

First published in Great Britain in 2020 by
Pen & Sword Transport
An imprint of
Pen & Sword Books Ltd
Yorkshire – Philadelphia

ISBN 978 1 52677 228 2

A CIP catalogue record for this book is
available from the British Library.

Typeset by Mac Style
Printed and bound in the UK by TJ Books Ltd,
Padstow, Cornwall.

Pen & Sword Books Limited incorporates the imprints of Atlas,
Archaeology, Aviation, Discovery, Family History, Fiction, History,
Maritime, Military, Military Classics, Politics, Select, Transport,
True Crime, Air World, Frontline Publishing, Leo Cooper, Remember
When, Seaforth Publishing, The Praetorian Press, Wharncliffe
Local History, Wharncliffe Transport, Wharncliffe True Crime
and White Owl.

For a complete list of Pen & Sword titles please contact

PEN & SWORD BOOKS LIMITED
47 Church Street, Barnsley, South Yorkshire, S70 2AS, England
E-mail: enquiries@pen-and-sword.co.uk
Website: www.pen-and-sword.co.uk

Or

PEN AND SWORD BOOKS
1950 Lawrence Rd, Havertown, PA 19083, USA
E-mail: Uspen-and-sword@casematepublishers.com
Website: www.penandswordbooks.com

To the staff of Queen's Hospital Romford and all NHS workers
This book shows the example of how Britain's railway workers went way beyond their normal duties to help the country through the crisis of the Second World War. The workers of the NHS have done the same in today's different kind of crisis and have led the way to enable the people of the UK to come through it.

Contents

Acknowledgements		viii
List of Illustrations		ix
Introduction		xv
Chapter 1	Military Railways	1
Chapter 2	Railways Before the Second World War	6
Chapter 3	1939	21
Chapter 4	1940	51
Chapter 5	1941	93
Chapter 6	1942	115
Chapter 7	1943	140
Chapter 8	1944	158
Chapter 9	1945	184
Chapter 10	Reflection	191
Afterword		194
Appendix I	*Second World War Railway Memorials*	198
Appendix II	*Commemorative Second World War Locomotives and Railway vehicles*	208
Glossary		213
Bibliography		214
Index		216

Acknowledgements

Thank you to the following for the use of their photographs: Lucy Colgrave, Kyra Foley, Neil Pruitt, Georgie Duane, Gillian Mawson, Linne Matthews and Mirrorpix.

Note on illustrations

Unless otherwise acknowledged, the pictures in this book are from the author's own collection of postcards, magazines and old photograph albums and it has been impossible to determine if any copyright is attached to them. Any infringement of copyright as a result of their publication is entirely unintentional; if any copyright has been infringed, the author extends his apologies to the parties concerned. Should this have happened, please contact the author through the publisher.

List of Illustrations

1. WWI army camp at Codford, Wiltshire, showing the purpose-built train line running into the camp.
2. Narrow gauge railway on the Western Front, supplying soldiers on the front line in WWI.
3. WWI army camp, location unknown, close to a railway line.
4. WWI service badges for employees of the LMS, GWR, LNER and SR.
5. Railway employees, some wearing their old army caps from WWI.
6. A King class engine being built at GWR's Swindon works.
7. Advertisement from the inter-war era for Continental holidays by train for the Southern Railway, featuring Sunny South Sam.
8. Pre-WWI image showing Bow Road station in London, once part of the Great Eastern Railway.
9. Newport Docks in South Wales, once owned by the GWR, from where men of the BEF left for France in WWI.
10. Barrow Docks, once owned by the LMS; the shipyards there were owned by Vickers, where they produced submarines during the war.
11. The SS *Great Western*, owned by the GWR. Built as a cargo ship, it was used as a troopship in 1944.
12. The *Flying Scotsman* – a Pacific class designed by Nigel Gresley and built at Doncaster in 1923. It was used on express routes mainly from London to Edinburgh.
13. *King George V* – a prototype of the King class of four-cylinder 4-6-0 passenger locomotives. Seen here pulling a GWR express from Bristol to Paddington.
14. A small LMS shunting engine, built by the Sentinel Wagon Works.
15. A steam engine at Euston.
16. Wartime advertisement showing how the railways were a vital link between shipping and factories.

17. Railway Executive Committee advertisement promoting the types of ticket that were available during the war.

18. A 'British Railways' blackout message aimed at making the public understand how difficult it was for railway staff and calling on the public to help.

19. Engine at sheds at Plaistow. The line through the station was once owned by the LMS but later became part of the District Line.

20. A train heading towards Shoeburyness – an experimental artillery site with its own railway system that was in use throughout the war as a coastal gunnery school.

21. Government information form explaining that accepting displaced persons into your home was not always a voluntary process during evacuation.

22. Members of the Boys' Brigade on a station platform, probably being evacuated although may have been going to camp.

23. Evacuees leaving Yarmouth station. (Gillian Mawson)

24. 'British Railways' advertisement promoting the wartime role of the railways.

25. 'British Railways' advertisement stating that armaments come first.

26. A Gloucester Wagon Company brake van.

27. Southampton Docks, which played a huge part in the war while owned by Southern Railways.

28. Pre-war advertisement for Southampton Docks – a vital part of Southern Railway's freight and passenger services.

29. A sleeper store at Hayes – one of a number of large railway equipment centres in the country before the war.

30. Victoria station memorial to the named men who died in WWI from the South Eastern & Chatham Railway Company. The plaque at the bottom mentions the men from Southern who died in WWII but does not list names.

31. Victoria station memorial naming the men of the London, Brighton & South Coast railway who died in WWI. The men of the Southern Railway who died in WWII are mentioned at the bottom of the plaque but are not named.

32. A list of docks owned by the railways in England, Scotland and Wales during the war.

33. The SS *St Helier*, built in 1925 for the GWR. It serviced the Channel Island routes before becoming a troopship in WWII, and then took part in the Dunkirk evacuation.

34. The *Great Bear* – a Pacific type 4-6-2 built at Swindon in 1908 for the GWR, converted into a Castle class 4-6-0 and renamed *Viscount Churchill* in 1924.

35. Paddington – a very busy passenger station with a very large indoor goods depot.

36. The Cornish Riviera Express, which would have carried many servicemen during the war.

37. Heysham Dock, owned by the LMS and used for ferries to Ireland and the Isle of Man. The nearby ICI factory was a target during the war.

38. Matchbox label asking the public to save coal during the war.

39. The SS *Isle of Guernsey*, built in 1930 for Southern Railway's route to the Channel Islands from Southampton. During the war, she carried RAF personnel to France, took part in the Dunkirk evacuation and carried Canadian troops on D-Day.

40. Dover – one of the most important of the south coast ports during the war and was taken over by the Admiralty.

41. Manchester Piccadilly memorial for those connected with the LMS who died in the war.

42. Soldiers on their way back from Dunkirk being given refreshments by volunteers. (Mirropix)

43. The *Tattersall Castle*, built in 1934 for the LNER's Humber ferry service. The ship carried soldiers across during the war and was one of first civilian ships to have radar.

44. Channel Islands evacuees leaving Crewe. (Courtesy of the Laine family/Gillian Mawson)

45. An LMS train in a London station after an attack.

46. One of the railway guns based at Dover and used to return fire on the German guns in France.

47. A train on the Glasgow Underground, where the tunnels were not deep enough to provide safe shelters.

48. Dover Priory station, which suffered constant damage from bombing and shelling throughout the war.

49. London Underground air raid shelter sign.
50. Bomb damage to a London station and the train in it.
51. London Underground air raid shelter sign advising that persons take shelter at their own risk.
52. People sleeping on the tracks in the London Underground.
53. Floodgates were fitted to a number of Underground stations in case bomb damage caused flooding. These can still be seen at Baker Street station.
54. Remembrance plaque at Balham Underground station, where, in October 1940 a bomb exploded, killing nearly seventy people.
55. Driver standing by LMS Ivatt locomotive No. 4423, built at Crewe.
56. A down train at Welshpool. Wales was one of the areas used as a reception point for a number of evacuees.
57. Railway Executive Committee advertisement explaining the vital work done by the railways during the war.
58. *Sarah Siddons* – one of the twenty old Vickers engines that ran on the Metropolitan Railway and were named after local celebrities. (Neil Pruitt)
59. Another view of the *Sarah Siddons* engine, which is now used for heritage events. (Georgie Duane)
60. One of the many Austerity locomotives built during the war – No. 8042, built for the LMS.
61. Moorgate in London was one of the stations that closed early in the war, in 1940, and remained closed until 1946.
62. Railway convalescent home at Dawlish, 1945.
63. A notice of changes to rail services in the north of England during evacuation. (Gillian Mawson)
64. A woman railway worker on signal duties during the war.
65. A GNR locomotive at Belfast Shed.
66. A Dundalk engine on the GNR in Northern Ireland.
67. Repair work taking place on the GWR at Lampton, Hounslow.
68. Railway war memorial in the bus station outside Euston station. (Kyra Foley)
69. A crowded station in London during the war, in spite of government attempts to stop the public travelling at holiday times.
70. Memorial to those who died at Blackpool Central station when an aircraft crashed on it after colliding with another aircraft.

71. Wartime military men travelling in a goods wagon.
72. Wartime railway staff at Faversham station.
73. War memorial at Paddington station. (Kyra Foley)
74. Naval men being issued with railway passes so they could go on leave.
75. Memorial to railway employees who died in both world wars at Edinburgh's Waverley station. (Linne Matthews)
76. The blockhouse built as an entrance to the air raid shelter at Clapham South station. (Kyra Foley)
77. Affluent passengers enjoying the comfort of dining and sleeper cars – a sharp contrast to how people travelled during the war.
78. The GWR railway works at Swindon – probably the largest in the world at the time.
79. Railway works being carried out at Totten, Hampshire.
80. A group of shunters – a dangerous job in wartime because of the blackout.
81. Engine No. 9022, built at Swindon, pulling a freight train at Whitechurch.
82. Wartime railway advertisement describing how 'British Railways' were 'carrying on'.
83. The wagon-building shed and sawmill at Swindon.
84. Mr Albert Taylor being presented with a gold medal by the mayor of Weston-super-Mare, Alderman Henry Butt, at the GWR ambulance class at Brown's café.
85. Advertisement publicising how the railways carried goods brought in by ship.
86. Two engines in a roofless shed at Tilbury Docks. The docks were active throughout the war, and boats left from there for Dunkirk.
87. Memorial outside Bethnal Green station, commemorating those killed in the wartime disaster.
88. Men of the Home Guard, who took over the job of guarding the railways from the regular army. A number of Home Guard units comprised railway employees.
89. War memorial inside King's Cross station, London.
90. The Blackpool to Manchester Victoria train at Bolton. The town was seriously damaged by wartime bombing.
91. Bomb-damaged Middleborough station in August 1942. (Mirrorpix)

92. One of the American locomotives that were shipped to Britain during the war, pictured here after D-Day, when it had been moved to France.

93. Horwich locomotive works, near Bolton, showing its own 18-inch gauge railway.

94. The Horwich works, which produced a number of different tanks for the army.

95. Train carrying Sherman tanks, probably on their way to a port in southern England ready to cross to Normandy. (Mirrorpix)

96. 1910 exhibition poster for Birmingham Railway Carriage & Wagon Co., Ltd., which produced railway equipment during WWII.

97. A bomb-damaged railway workshop, location unknown.

98. Unloading locomotives that had been transported from America.

99. Military railway voucher for prisoners of war.

100. Southern Railway third class carriage.

101. A throat plate being pressed in Swindon's railway workshop.

102. Blue plaque at Stockport station commemorating the arrival of evacuees from the Channel Islands.(Gilliam Mawson)

103. Hythe Station on the Romney, Hythe and Dymchurch Railway, which was taken over by the military in WWII.

104. *Thomas the Tank Engine* on the Watercress Line, the Mid-Hants Railway, which played an important part in the war as it ran from Aldershot to Southampton. (Lucy Colgrove)

Introduction

The outbreak of the Second World War was of little surprise to most people as it had been expected for some time. In relation to the railway system in Britain, this was evident in their pre-war preparations and training for such things as air raids and gas attacks. Railway staff were the first non-military group to be supplied with steel helmets, which demonstrates how important the railways were going to be during the conflict.

The war period is a fascinating part of our history and, as time goes on, there will be fewer and fewer people with first-hand memories of it. This was one of the reasons I wanted to write this book, together with my lifelong interest in the railways and the vital role they played in supporting their country in wartime – a role, I believe, that is often overlooked.

The challenges faced by the railways in Britain during the Second World War were very different to those they had faced during the First World War. In that war, most of Britain's troops were fighting abroad for the whole of the conflict so were not routinely transported around the country in large numbers, apart from moving from one camp to another. The railway system at that time consisted of hundreds of different companies. Although this had changed by the outbreak of the Second World War, the Big Four railway companies that had been formed from mergers and takeovers were not used to working together.

After the fall of France in the Second World War, the British Army, along with troops from around the empire and other European countries, were based in Britain and were later reinforced by the arrival of US troops. This meant that throughout the war there was a constant need to transport large numbers of soldiers, especially after the evacuation from Dunkirk, which took place from 26 May to 4 June 1940, and the period leading up to D-Day, 6 June 1944.

Moving these military men and equipment around was no easy task. This could range from small parties of men on a regular passenger train to a huge number of troops needing 300 special trains, or an item of equipment in a single wagon to fifty trains carrying tanks and armoured vehicles – and all needing to be done at a moment's notice while also running a 'normal' railway service.

The railway service, of course, was far from normal during the conflict. Wartime production in the nation's factories was vastly increased to provide the men of the armed forces with the munitions they needed to fight the war. The increase in production was a major step up from the decline that had taken place in many industries in the interwar years. The railways were not only responsible for delivering raw materials to industrial units but were also needed to move finished, often dangerous, loads from the factories to their final destination. There was also a major increase in the number of factories required to supply war needs. Many of these new factories were enormous, built in remote areas that needed railways to bring in the building materials for their construction and then

1. The early First World War army camps were mainly built in remote areas. Many had their own train lines running into the camp, usually built by the Royal Engineers. This one shows Codford Camp in Wiltshire.

to transport raw materials and finished goods back and forth. They also had to carry the employees to the new works and home again at various times due to the number of shifts needed to keep the factories in operation day and night.

Operating the railways during the Second World War was vastly different to running a railway during peacetime. Everyone is aware that even nowadays, trains can be halted by the 'wrong kind of snow', and the winter of 1939/40 saw the worst kind of snow in terms of quantity and prolonged frosts. Indeed, it seemed that the all the winters during the war years were so much more severe than they had been in peacetime.

After struggling through that first winter, the wartime railways then had to face attacks by the German Air Force as the bombing got under way. In coastal towns, such as Dover, enemy aircraft dealt out death and destruction in alarming regularity, but after the evacuation of Dunkirk, there was the additional hazard of long-range shelling from the coast of France. Railway workers also had to endure the constant fear of danger as they were often in the target zone of the German bombers and machine-gunners, sadly evidenced by the number of fatalities.

Then there were the difficulties of the blackout. Large marshalling yards often had to deal with as many as 2,000 trucks in a single night. This would have been hard enough to deal with in the normal lamplit darkness but during the blackout, one can only imagine what it was like when wagons suddenly appeared out of the gloom only perhaps a few feet away from men working in the yards before they could be seen.

One of the other tasks that the railways had to cope with was the evacuation of children from the towns and cities most at risk of bombing and coastal locations thought to be at risk of invasion. The difficulty in anticipating when the bombs would arrive meant that there was no single movement of those being evacuated. When the predicted early bombing raids didn't materialise, many children who had been involved in the first wave of evacuation came home, only to be moved again when the bombing actually began. There followed further waves of evacuation as the V-1 flying bombs and V-2 rockets targeted South East England in the later years of the war.

Those who were running the railways in wartime also had to deal with the issue of civilians who wanted or needed to travel, although there were constant government appeals to the public not to do so. The appeals seemed to have been largely ignored, especially during holiday times. The government promoted the concept of Stay at Home holidays, but traditional holiday periods often turned out to be very busy, with people trying as best they could to seek pleasure away from home and escape the long hours spent in munitions factories. There were even cases of holidaymakers trying to use the railways to get to coastal areas that had been closed to the public.

The railway system faced all of these pressures with one hand tied behind its back. The shortage of workers began to bite as the call for men to join the forces increased. Luckily, the nation's women stepped up to take their place. It wasn't as easy to replace the ageing and often badly damaged rolling stock. Building army tanks often took precedence over new locomotives in the railway workshops, and many of the engines being used dated from the nineteenth century and would in ordinary times have been taken out of commission.

Alongside details of how the railways coped with the major events of the conflict, I have included more personal stories as they often reveal things that are more usually overlooked. One example of this is from the later stages of the war when trains were carrying American troops. In Britain, there were shortages of everything. This was not so amongst American servicemen, who were often careless with their ample supplies, providing a bonus for the railway staff who had to clear up after them.

These small details are told as much by the images in the book as the text. For instance, despite the government attempting to restrict use of the railways by the public, they continued to travel. There are images of members of the Boys' Brigade waiting on the platform to travel to camp as well as photographs of stations crowded with passengers who were defying government instructions.

Considering the problems the railways faced, it is a wonder that they managed to get through the war at all. This is the story of how they did it.

Chapter 1

Military Railways

It is a surprising fact that the British military, who were normally so averse to accepting new ideas or technology even as late as the First World War, were eager to use the railway system from the mid-nineteenth century. The public at home had been horrified to learn of the condition of British troops in Crimea, which was widely reported in *The Times* and was mainly due to the difficulty of moving supplies to the front because of the terrible road conditions in the area.

It was a man named Samuel Morton Peto who exerted a great influence on the military in accepting the new technology and so changed conditions for the better for the British troops. Peto had been involved in the building of the Great Western Railway, and under the direction of the Secretary of State for War, the Duke of Newcastle, was responsible for building a railway from Balaclava to Sebastopol. The 7-mile line was completed in just over seven weeks and was of a standard gauge of 4 feet 8½ inches. It was due to the capability of the line in bringing up supplies that the siege of Sebastopol was successful. The line was also the first to be used by a hospital train.

The Crimean War was a turning point in military history as it was realised that the army needed more than just fighting men. It also needed a properly organised level of services, which led to the formation of the Land Transport Corps, the forerunner of the Royal Corps of Transport. However, this wasn't easy to achieve. The Land Transport Corps were disbanded as soon as the war ended. There was then some dispute over the fact that the officers of the corps were seen as part of a civilian rather than a military organisation.

According to an article in the *Hampshire Chronicle* in 1856, a new corps, the Military Train, was being created, which would become a permanent department of the army. Its duties would be to convey all stores, ammunition and equipment. It was to be formed from the most eligible volunteers of the disbanded Land Transport Corps.

In a later development, the Engineer and Railway Staff Corps, affiliated to the Royal Engineers, was founded in 1865. The aim of this corps was to ensure that all the railway companies took combined action when the country faced danger. Before a war began, they were to prepare schemes for transporting troops to areas where they were needed. This meant that for most of the time they were in existence, they had hardly anything to do. The corps were also unique in consisting entirely of officers.

The success of the Crimean railway line obviously had an influence on military tactics. In 1896, Sirdar Horatio Kitchener was responsible for the construction of the Sudan Military Railroad during the Mahdist War, which was built to supply the Anglo-Egyptian army. Although the line was part of a planned railway, it was created purely for military purposes rather than for bringing civilisation to the area, although it later became part of the Sudan Railway.

Lord Cromer had agreed the building of the railway but expected it to be a cheaper, narrow gauge construction of 2 feet or 2 feet 6 inches. Instead, Kitchener, who had previously met Cecil Rhodes, built a line that was of a 3-foot 6-inch gauge. Rhodes had already begun to build a railway of similar gauge between Kimberley and Bulawayo.

Previous to this, the first Royal Engineers Railway Company had been formed in 1882. They were involved in the Mahdist War in Egypt, and also later in the Sudan. When they returned from the Sudan, the new company was based at the Chattenden and Upnor Railway, close to the Royal Engineers' headquarters at Chatham.

As well as the British Army's growing awareness of the vital role of the railways during times of conflict, there were other examples of military use in the nineteenth century. The railway proved effective in the American Civil War, particularly in the use of armoured trains.

The new British Army Corps of Royal Engineers was active during the Second Boer War (1899–1902). Armoured trains were a new feature of the conflict for the British, although were not to prove as effective as was hoped. This was shown on 15 November 1899, when Winston Churchill, acting as a correspondent for the *Morning Post*, joined a scouting expedition on an armoured train. The train was captured by the Boers and Churchill became a prisoner of war for a brief period before managing to escape in mid-December.

After the Boer War, the Royal Engineers Railway Company returned to Chattenden before moving to Longmoor, Hampshire, in 1905.

The early success of the first military railways led to the development of narrow gauge railways during the First World War. There were a number of these built to supply the forces on the Western Front, often carrying supplies across land unusable by any other form of transport.

The greatest success of the railways in the First World War was evident when the Americans arrived. The British and the French asked the Americans to organise nine Railway Engineer units in 1917. There were 1,065 men in each unit; some were construction teams, others were workshop units. After a call for men working in other army units who had railway experience, many of the railwaymen went to Europe.

The Americans operated US trains on the French railway system. They then set up narrow gauge railways leading from railheads to the front line. The trench railways were 60-centimetre gauge (23⅝ inches). There were 7 to 10 miles of railway for each mile of the front. The engines were mainly steam but there were also diesel engines near the front to avoid the enemy spotting the steam from the other engines.

It wasn't only on the front line that military railways were of use. As the military camps back in Britain began to grow in size, they often had

2. The use of railways by the army increased greatly in the First World War. On the Western Front, narrow gauge railways were the only efficient way to supply the men on the front line.

their own branch lines built to carry new recruits to their training centres. As the need for more men became acute, the size of training camps grew until those such as the enormous establishment at Clipstone, near Mansfield in Nottinghamshire, became common. Clipstone expanded to hold thousands of men, although most of the early arrivals left the train at Edwinstone station and marched to the camp. This was despite the fact that sidings had been built to the camp on which goods trains were used to deliver supplies. It appears that trains were considered better employed to carry military supplies than to carry the men.

Many of the early military camps of the First World War era were built in remote places. This was the case with RAF Cranwell, Lincolnshire, when it opened as a Royal Naval Air Service base in 1915. It soon became apparent that road transportation of bulk supplies to the camp from Sleaford wasn't practical. A railway line was needed but there was some dispute over who should build it: the Board of Trade or the Admiralty? It was eventually paid for by the Admiralty.

The army were building their own railways and by 1914 there were two regular and three reserve Royal Engineers Railway Companies. These men were sent to France to build the railways to the front, along with Labour Companies to act as navvies.

3. An army camp close to a railway line, location unknown.

The Railway Executive Committee was responsible for recruiting substantial numbers of employees from the larger railway companies in Britain for these units. Around half the officers for the reserve units were from the rail companies. The rest were from overseas railway companies. Some of the men serving in the same companies were recruited together and formed pals units, although this tailed off as the size of the RE Railway Company grew.

At the end of the First World War, many of the locomotives used in France were returned to Britain and put into storage, where they were forgotten and left to deteriorate. Many of these had been built by companies such as Hunslet, Kerr Stuart and Alco for specific use on the narrow gauge railways on the Western Front. Being left to rot was a waste of engines that in most cases were only a few years old and could have been used elsewhere.

The headquarters of the railway companies was still at Longmoor, where the reserve companies trained every year between the wars using the Woolmer Military Railway.

There were some historic military train connections at Shoeburyness Artillery Barracks in Essex up to the late twentieth century. The camp had its own railway system and they were given the Kitchener Coach, which had been built by the Metropolitan Carriage and Wagon Company in Birmingham in 1885 for Kitchener's Suakin-Berber military railway that was constructed in the Sudan. The railway was never finished and closed soon after it was begun. There was a parliamentary scandal about the railway, so the War Department decided to bring back all the railway vehicles, including Kitchener's Coach. There is some doubt as to whether Kitchener used it much but it has retained his name. At Shoeburyness, this coach was used to entertain dignitaries visiting the site. When Shoeburyness closed, the coach went to the Museum of Army Transport at Beverley, in Yorkshire. When this museum closed, the coach was moved to the Royal Engineers Museum at Gillingham, in Kent, and then to Chatham Historic Dockyard, where it remains on display.

By the time the Second World War began, it was not only the civilian railways that were to play a part in the conflict. Alongside this was a better organised military railway group, which worked with the main railway companies while using their skills to provide transport for the Allied forces in many parts of the world.

Chapter 2

Railways Before the Second World War

The early railway system was a collection of hundreds of small companies that sprang up from the 1830s onwards, with the smaller ones being successively swallowed up by those that prospered more quickly. From the conception of the railways as a form of transport, each company was legislated by its own Act of Parliament. By the mid-nineteenth century, Parliament had agreed the building of nearly 300 railways, although not all of them were completed.

The cost of constructing a railway depended on the part of the country in which it was situated. The more difficult terrains incurred extra expense, which often led to the collapse of the company. Consequently, by the time of the outbreak of the First World War, there were about 120 railway companies in Britain.

The railway system continued to expand, with the larger companies acquiring the smaller ones, although a number of small railway companies maintained their independence, even when the government took control during the war. After the war ended, the railways came close to being nationalised, a threat that was to hang over them for years.

When Eric Campbell Geddes put forward his Cabinet paper in 1921, he suggested that the railways in Britain be formed into five or six groups. The Railways Act 1921 came into force on 1 January 1923 and the newly amalgamated companies became known as the 'Big Four' – a name coined by the *Railway Magazine* in February 1923. These were the Great Western Railway (GWR), the London and North Eastern Railway (LNER), the London, Midland and Scottish Railway (LMS) and the Southern Railway (SR) companies. There was also a separate London Passenger Transport Board.

Competition between the Big Four was evident. There had been a time when no railway company would dare to allow a train to trespass on to another company's lines. In America there was an incident of this happening, resulting in the tracks of the connecting line being pulled up to stop the offending train returning to its own lines. There is a rumour that this once happened in Britain, although there is no direct evidence of it. By the outbreak of the Second World War, there was a great deal of co-operation, with tolerance of trains using other companies' tracks.

The London, Midland and Scottish Railway was claimed to be the largest transport organisation in Europe. Before the war, the company operated more than 7,000 miles of track across the UK. It was the only British railway company to serve England, Scotland, Ireland and Wales. They also had a chain of twenty-eight hotels, twenty-five docks, harbours and piers, a number of large engineering workshops, and sixty-six steamships, as well as owning thousands of houses. They were more concerned with carrying freight than passengers. The two main

4. Railway service badges were of twofold use during the war. They showed that a man was working on the railway and not shirking his duty by avoiding service in the forces, and they were also a way of recognising employees at security conscious railway depots. Here are examples of employees' badges for each of the Big Four: the Great Western Railway; the London, Midland and Scottish Railway; the London North Eastern Railway; and the Southern Railway.

constituents of the LMS were the Midland Railway and the North West Railway, which had previously been strong rivals.

In the early 1930s, William Arthur Stanier was appointed Chief Mechanical Engineer of the LMS. He was responsible for introducing new types of locomotives with many distinctive advances that were regarded as revolutionary. One of these was the taper pattern boiler, in which the water space was smaller at the smokebox end, where the heat transmission through the tubes was lowest. The water space was greater at the firebox end, where it was needed most. This also meant that there was a saving of weight at the smokebox end on the carrying wheels.

The company owned more than 7,000 locomotives, including the most powerful of those run by the Big Four – thirty-three Beyer Garratts, which had a tractive effort of 45,620lb and were built in the late 1930s.

The LMS also operated a number of electric lines, mainly in the London area. These were from Euston to Watford and Richmond, and had been in operation since before the First World War, although at that time the lines had been run by the London and North Western Railway (L&NWR).

The London and North Eastern Railway controlled 6,500 miles of track, which included the East Coast Main Line (ECML) from London to Edinburgh. The LNER was responsible for carrying much of the

5. A group of railway employees, some of whom appear to be wearing their old army caps, probably from the First World War.

country's coal supplies, although it also operated as a transport system carrying passengers to holiday destinations – a service glamorously portrayed in its advertising posters by graphic artists such as Tom Purvis.

The LNER had an unusual record in owning the largest railway wagon in Great Britain. It had fifty-six wheels and could carry a load of 150 tons. The company also held the record for the longest nonstop run from London to Edinburgh, a distance of 392 miles, made by the *Flying Scotsman* on 1 May 1928. They also gained the world speed record for a steam railway locomotive when, on 3 July 1938, the *Mallard* ran for 5 miles above 120 mph and reached a top speed of 126 mph.

At the outbreak of the Second World War, the LNER had no electrified lines in London, although there had been some work towards electrifying the lines between Liverpool Street and Shenfield, and there were plans to electrify the Manchester to Sheffield main line.

The Great Western Railway was unusual in that it started off as a broad gauge system. This was mainly due to Isambard Kingdom Brunel, who built the railway without any regard for the fact that one day, railways would have to co-operate. His 7-foot gauge was opposed to most other railways, which had a standard gauge of 4 feet 8½ inches. The few other railways that adopted broad gauge were later taken over by the GWR.

The GWR was different from the other members of the Big Four in that it absorbed a number of smaller companies in 1921, whereas the other three amalgamated with two or more track lines. It was the only one of the Big Four to have kept its original name from its inception.

The GWR controlled only 3,800 miles of track and was a large carrier of coal, mainly from Wales. At one time, the company led the way in its stock of locomotives with the Castle and King classes, which were able to set several records for speed. They were designed by C.B. Collett and produced at their Swindon works. By the late 1930s, the Swindon works were producing Castle, Hall Grange and Manor type engines. It was claimed to be the largest and most up-to-date railway works in the world for the construction of engines, carriages and wagons, and produced 100 new locomotives a year.

The GWR's connection with Swindon is a long one that has had a great influence on the town. Not only did it bring employment to the area, but from the mid-nineteenth century, it had a fund that provided

6. A King class engine being built at GWR's Swindon works. The King class were introduced in 1927 for express passenger work and were the company's largest, most powerful engines at that time.

medical care for the workers and their families and was supposedly the model on which the National Health Service was based.

The Southern Railway Company was the smallest of the Big Four, with just over 2,000 miles of track concentrated in the south of England, with no lines north of London. It nevertheless matched the other companies in terms of passengers, carrying almost a quarter of the country's rail travellers as it operated mainly as a passenger railway. This was understandable as it serviced many of the most densely populated areas around the capital.

The Southern was divided into three sections: the Western, which had been mainly the London and South Western Railway; the Central, which had been the Brighton Railway; and the Eastern, which had been the South Eastern and Chatham Railway. The company had a number of London termini, including Waterloo – the largest passenger station in the country, with twenty-one platforms.

London had one of the densest levels of passenger traffic in the world. In the period just before the Second World War, the majority of passenger trains on the Southern Railway that terminated within 30 miles of London were electric. The coastal services between Hastings and Portsmouth were also electric. Electric trains were not popular with everyone. According to railway historian W.G. Tilling, writing in 1943, they were 'lifeless things that glide at the same pace uphill or down without effort or interest to those who watch'. Steam was obviously more his cup of tea.

Southern was also very successful in promoting itself, with well-known slogans and a character called 'Sunny South Sam', who appeared on their advertisements. It was also one of the first of the Big Four to move towards widespread electrification of its lines. By the beginning of the war, more than 1,700 miles of Southern's passenger lines had been electrified.

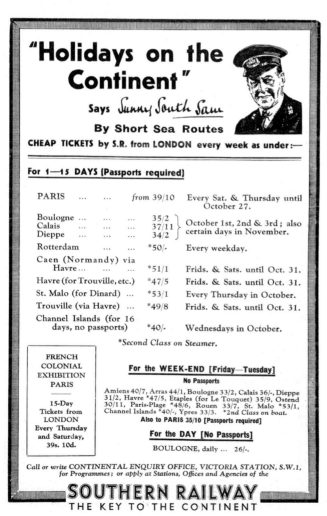

7. The pre-war railway companies tried to give an impression of their services being romantic and upmarket. Southern had a well-known character who appeared on their advertisements: Sunny South Sam.

The Southern had been developed mainly as a passenger railway as there were no early centres of industry in the area it covered. It was only the discovery of coal in Kent in 1890 that prompted a more industrial development.

Rail transport in London was a separate matter, with the London Underground Electric Railway and the Metropolitan Line, which were both independent of the Big Four. The lines were often undercut by cheap buses and in 1933 they came under the control of the London Passenger Transport Board, which also controlled the buses.

Many of the stations on the Underground today that are solely part of London Transport were once on adjoining railway companies' stations or on separate lines belonging to different companies. Many of the overground parts of the London Transport system were separate lines run by other companies and not part of the Underground system at all. Because of the number of different companies, many stations were built that were close to others and were not really needed when the London system was unified.

The idea of the London Underground was formed in the mid-nineteenth century but it was the early twentieth century that was to see its real progress. In 1902, the Underground Electric Railways Company of London Limited (UERL) was established. The plan of the company

8. Not all of the railway lines in London were part of the London Transport system. This old image shows that Bow Road was once part of the Great Eastern Railway.

was to electrify the District Line, and the first part of the electrification between Ealing and Harrow was carried out the following year.

The London Underground system came into being in 1933, after the London Passenger Transport Act. The London Passenger Transport Board (LPTB) took over control of all passenger transport services in London except the lines still owned by mainline companies. The Board did have control of the Metropolitan, District, London Electric, South London and Central London lines – in all, 128 miles of track. They owned sixty-three locomotives and 2,951 passenger vehicles.

There were some railways that remained independent of the Big Four after 1923, including a number of light railways. Many of these were originally built to carry freight such as coal or stone and were later used for passengers. A number were controlled by Colonel Holman Fred Stevens, who was a civil engineer and manager. At one point he managed sixteen of these railways in England and Wales. Many light railways survived well into the twentieth century and a few of them, such as the East Kent Light Railway and the Ffestiniog Railway, are now operating as heritage railways.

The railway companies also owned something else that was to be a vital resource during the Second World War – about 95 miles of dockside quays. The LMS was the largest wharf owner in Britain. The railways did not, however, own the large docks at London, Liverpool and Glasgow.

9. Newport Docks in South Wales were owned by the GWR and played an early part in WWII when men of the BEF left from there for France. In return, the area was bombed the following year.

10. Barrow Docks were owned by the LMS but the shipyards were owned by Vickers, who produced a number of submarines there during the war.

Barrow Docks comprise 300 acres of water space and 400 acres of quay space, equipped with warehouses and sheds for storage of grain and other traffic. Large areas are available for storage of timber, minerals, ores, etc. Steam, hydraulic and electric cranes are available for all classes of lifts. The LMS perform stevedoring services, and all berths are rail-connected. Extensive water space is available for the laying up of idle shipping and for storage of floating timber. Excellent rail-connections with all parts of the country. Average annual volume of traffic 375,000 tons.

L M S

BARROW

Full information from F. K. Rogers, District Goods and Passenger Manager, LMS Railway, Barrow-in-Furness, or Ashton Davies, Chief Commercial Manager, LMS Railway, Euston Station, N.W.1.

DOCKS

The railway companies also owned 130 steamships, which were used on numerous routes depending on which company owned them, including Ireland, Scottish islands, the Channel Islands, France and the Netherlands. These ships were mainly taken over by the Admiralty during the war rather than being controlled by the Railway Executive Committee.

The takeover of the railways in the UK for the period of the Second World War was not a completely new experience. The same thing had happened during the First World War, when the country's railways were run by the Railway Executive Committee, and the experience revealed that having fewer companies in control of the rail system was

11. The SS *Great Western* was the third ship of that name owned by the GWR. She was built by Cammell Laird mainly as a cargo ship and used as a troopship in 1944.

an advantage. There was some consideration given to nationalising the railways at this time – an idea that had first been put forward in the mid-nineteenth century.

The Big Four had continued to develop their own systems throughout the interwar period, with improvements to the lines and rolling stock. As well as more modern locomotives they also introduced more luxurious carriages and restaurant cars.

The express services that the railway companies were running were the most luxurious form of travel in the UK and included trains such as the GWR's Cheltenham Flyer and Cornish Rivera Express; the LNER's Coronation; the LMS's Royal Scot and Coronation Scot; and the SR's Atlantic Coast Express and Golden Arrow. There were almost 400 sleeping cars and 900 restaurant cars across the four railway companies.

Further improvements in services saw the introduction of electric cookers and refrigeration to the catering facilities. Many of the 100 express trains were capable of serving 200 meals at once. Of course, the opportunity to travel on these trains and enjoy the first class services was only available to the better off members of the travelling public.

For those who could not afford the luxury of first class, cheaper options were available. The LNER had introduced third class sleeping cars,

12. *Flying Scotsman* is arguably the best known locomotive in the world. It is a Pacific class, desgined by Nigel Gresley and built at Doncaster in 1923. It was used on express routes mainly from London to Edinburgh. *Flying Scotsman* was the first engine to reach 100mph. During the war it was painted black, like other engines, and painted green again after the war. It is still running today, despite once being in danger of being scrapped, and appears at numerous locations.

which had already been available on the GWR and the LMS. The LNER sleeping class were convertible back to normal third class coaches if not needed for overnight accommodation, but the company had introduced ten new, exclusive third class sleepers. These had been designed by Mr H.N. Gresley and built at York.

Freight services could offer next-day delivery of items to places 300 miles apart, and the railways provided the largest household removal

13. *King George V* was a prototype of the King class of four-cylinder 4-6-0 passenger locomotives. It is seen here pulling one of the GWR expresses from Bristol to Paddington. Both places suffered extensively from bombing during the war.

service in the country. Where new factories were built, it was possible for them to acquire their own sidings – proving a vital element to the war service. Through the 1930s, however, there had been some loss of freight due to an increasing level of road traffic.

There had also been some major developments in train design in the years leading up to the Second World War. One of these was an increasing use of diesel instead of coal. Experiments determined that diesel was better suited to shunting engines and the LMS had ordered nine diesel shunting engines in the early 1930s. In order to try all that were available, there were eight different types amongst these nine engines. The two that were the same were Hudswell Clarke machines, and these needed modifications. The diesel locos were so successful that another twenty were ordered the following year. The LMS also had three diesel Leyland rail cars that were used for passenger trains. Although intended for short journeys, they were successfully trialled over longer distances.

The interwar period also saw a move towards a more sober design for railway stations. The railways had been developed in a romantic age and their buildings reflected this. For example, St Pancras station in London, built in the 1860s, is of Victorian Gothic design, and Sheffield station,

14. A small LMS shunting engine, built by the Sentinel Wagon Works at Shrewsbury, Shropshire. The early versions of the locomotive were single speed.

opened in 1870, looked more like a castle than a railway station. Hillside station opened in 1926, on the ex-Lancashire and Yorkshire Railway, which was by this time part of the LMS. The station building is small and of a very plain construction, which reflected the economic downturn of the 1920s. The decline in the previous grand architecture of the railways was evident in the new stations on the expanding London Underground between the wars. St John's Wood and Swiss Cottage stations were opened in 1939 as part of the Bakerloo extension. Their entrances were quite plain and have since been amalgamated into parts of much larger buildings. St John's Wood station, however, has now become a Grade II listed building in its own right.

One of the biggest improvements in the railways at this time was in the speed of trains. By 1937, Britain's trains were amongst the fastest in the world, with streamlined expresses averaging 80 miles per hour over a distance. Not everyone agreed that this was actually an improvement. According to *Railway Magazine*, some people were uneasy about the speed stunts that had become fashionable between the wars.

There was serious interest in the maximum speed attainable by steam, although the potential dangers were regarded as posing a great risk to passengers and railway workers. There was, of course, some basis for this

15. An engine at Euston, showing how much steam old locomotives produced.

as when travelling at such great speeds, there was less time to see the signals and stop in an emergency.

As well as the development of faster trains, from 1937 there were other advances in rail transport. Many of the railway workshops had moved away from predominantly making and repairing locomotives and wagons. A number of them were now turning their hand to military hardware. Railway employees were undertaking gas training, and wagonloads of explosives were being moved to war-ready stations around the country. Many of the preparations carried out in 1937 appeared to be redundant after the Munich Agreement of September 1938, and it looked like the railways could return to their primary role of carrying passengers and freight.

The preparations for war did not stop altogether, though. Training for dealing with gas and bomb attacks continued. Many of the breakdown trains were fitted with special equipment for decontamination, although thankfully, this was never put to the test. There was more investment in equipment for dealing with peacetime railway accidents and the number of breakdown trains was increased. Spare tracks, sleepers and other equipment had previously been kept in large central stores, but now, smaller supplies of these essentials were moved to a larger number of repair centres.

Perhaps the most important preparation took place in September 1938 when the Railway Executive Committee was formed, with the purpose of taking full control of the railways on the outbreak of war. At that point, there were probably only a few who had any doubt that war would come in the near future. The early formation of the committee gave them the opportunity to meet and discuss what would happen when the time came rather than being thrown into a situation with no time to prepare.

Chapter 3

1939

It had become evident to the military authorities that a reliable and large enough transport system was a vital necessity during wartime. This had proved to be the case in all the wars that Britain had fought since the railway came into existence, and government control of the railways during the First World War had provided the experience and understanding of what would be needed in another war.

The Railway Executive Committee was to work under the direction of the Ministry of Transport. It was initially an advisory body responsible for co-ordinating emergency plans for the railways, with its headquarters at Fielden House in Westminster.

The main objective of the committee was to take control of the Big Four railway companies. There were still, however, the other rail companies that had never become part of the Big Four. In many cases these were small light railways, but some were bigger, such as the East Kent Light Railway, which joined the Kent coalfields to the Southern. There were also the Kent and East Sussex Light Railway, which was used for moving agricultural traffic in the Rother Valley; the King's Lynn Docks and Railway Company; and the Mersey Railway, which was a similar service to the London Underground, but for Liverpool and Birkenhead. The Mersey was the second-oldest underground railway in the world after London. The Shropshire and Montgomeryshire Light Railway connected Wales with the Staffordshire potteries.

The adoption of the railway system by the government led to the setting up of a number of committees, which is the norm in any government-controlled establishment. There were regional transport committees, port emergency committees, railway traffic officers, railway liaison officers and many others. It was a complete civil service for transport.

While the railways were under the control of the state, their revenues were paid to the government, who then made a fixed payment of

£40 million per year back to the railways. Before the war, the railways had not been financially sound. Only one of the companies had paid a dividend to shareholders in 1938, and that had only been a half per cent. The amount the government was paying them was more than the companies had earned in the year before the war began. The price of railway shares increased significantly after the government deal.

While the Big Four planned to move their head offices out of London in the event of war (the LMS to Watford, the GWR to Aldermaston, the SR to Deepdene and the LNER to Hitchin), the Railway Executive Committee stayed in the capital to be close to the government. When war did break out, they moved to Down Street Underground station, which was considered bombproof. The station was still passed by trains on the Victoria Line but secret offices and dormitories were built there for the committee members. The committee members were allowed to stop trains passing through to travel to the next station.

It was on 1 September 1939 that the government took over the railways, two days before war was declared, and the Railway Executive Committee was then in control for the duration of the conflict. Although this was a national organisation, there was some local involvement when it came to the carrying of freight. This was organised by the Ministry of Supply but there were a number of Regional Transport Committees, who had useful local knowledge.

The
VITAL
LINK

RAILWAYS are the vital link between the convoys with their urgent and important freights and the factories waiting for the materials to make the weapons of war.
Railways are also the essential link between the factories and the battle. They play a major part in every Allied campaign and are of paramount importance in the strategy of modern war.
Few, if any, other sections of industry have had to undertake a task so immensely increased in volume.

BRITISH **RAILWAYS**
GWR · LMS   LNER · SR

Carrying the War Load

16. A wartime advertisement showing how the railways were a vital link between shipping and factories. It seems to have been more of a propaganda message than an advertisement.

The Big Four did, however, retain some of their own character, as Bernard Darwin, in his 1946 book *War on the Line*, explained: 'Despite the united effort of the war they [the Big Four] did not lose their own entities and character.' This was evident at places such as Manchester London Road station (now Piccadilly). The station was shared by the LNER and the LMS. The LNER platforms were lettered ABC, whilst the LMS were numbered. This was maintained during the war to avoid confusion.

The government also took over the running of the London Passenger Transport Board, the East Kent Light Railway, the Kent and East Sussex Light Railway, the King's Lynn Docks and Railway Company, the Mersey Railway Company and the Shropshire and Montgomeryshire Light Railway Company. The Railway Executive Committee consisted of Sir Ralph Wedgwood as chairman, Sir James Milner, Mr C.H. Newton, Mr Frank Pick, Mr Gilbert Szlumper and Sir William Wood.

It was during this period that the title British Rail was first used – a sign of what was to come after the end of the war. Railway posters (many designed by Fred Taylor, one of Britain's foremost railway artists), which had done so much to promote rail travel in the pre-war period, were now employed to do the exact opposite. People were dissuaded from travelling on the railways as the system was needed for a far more important role.

There were posters that requested the population holidayed at home rather than travel elsewhere in the country. As the war went on, many coastal areas became closed to visitors anyway, but the countryside was still open. Other posters promoted military use over public use, for example the one titled 'All clear for the guns', showing a passenger train waiting to allow a freight train loaded with guns to go first.

The railways expected to be bombed, so to protect their workers and passengers there was some industrious shelter building. As well as building shelters, the LMS also dug trenches for their staff in which to take cover. There was even an idea that old engine boiler barrels could be used as protection. Railway staff were given gas masks and were the first members of the public to be issued with helmets. Staff at this time were those who were left after others had been called up or volunteered for service, or had found higher pay in munitions factories.

Rail travel for the public wasn't easy under the Railway Executive Committee during the conflict. Trains were terribly overcrowded and delays could be very long. There were also the problems of station names being removed, the lack of buffet cars, and dimly lit carriages due to the blackout.

During peacetime, even though the railways ran twenty-four hours a day, seven days a week, most factories only worked a five-and-a-half-day week. This changed during the war as factories worked shifts throughout the day and night, as well as at weekends, to meet the demands of the war, so the railways had to adapt to accommodate the extra journeys for workers that this incurred.

Although the blackout was strictly enforced on most aspects of the railways, there were problems with signal boxes. They were a unique type of building with wide windows to give a clear view of the lines they controlled. There was no way that the light in the signal box could be reduced enough to comply with blackout regulations as it would restrict the ability of the signalman to operate safely.

SERVING YOU STILL...

In spite of the heavy National demands on the Railways, passengers by train can *still* obtain :—

- Cheap day tickets
- Monthly return and week-end tickets
- Season tickets
- Traders' tickets
- Workmen's tickets
- Walking Tour Tickets

Full particulars of the services being operated are obtainable at any railway station, office or agency.

The British Railways are carrying on.

Issued by

THE RAILWAY EXECUTIVE COMMITTEE

17. While the government was trying to deter the public from travelling on the railways during the war, the railway companies were still advertising the types of tickets that were still available.

A number of experiments were carried out, including the use of ultraviolet rays and levers covered with fluorescent paint. This didn't work so it was decided that the only possible solution was that light was shaded off the windows and reduced to the minimum necessary for safe operation of the box. Signalmen were also given large metal boxes in which to shelter during air raids; because of the large windows, flying glass was a significant danger.

HAS IT EVER OCCURRED TO YOU

THAT THE STATION STAFF WORK UNDER GREAT DIFFICULTIES

WHEN YOU TRAVEL IN THE BLACKOUT .

Arrive in good time for your train.

Please have your ticket ready at the barrier.

Travel light.

Tell your fellow passengers the names of the stations.

Close the carriage door after you.

HELP THE RAILWAYS TO HELP YOU

BRITISH RAILWAYS

G W R — L M S — L N E R — S R

18. A blackout message to raise awareness of the difficulties that railway staff were facing, and calling on the public to help.

Railway staff were given instructions on what to do in case of an air raid on a train, and these also applied to passengers. If the train stopped outside a station, they were told not to get off. They were to shut the blinds, even in daytime, as this could protect them from flying glass, and lay on the floor if there was room.

There were a number of scare stories concerning the railways and the war. There was, for instance, a notion that railway lines could be used to guide enemy aircraft from one place to another, although there was an overestimation of how easily this could be done by pilots in bombers that often flew at very high altitude.

There has been much written about how women played a large part in the work of the railways during the war but this was not to happen in a big way until the National Service Act of 1941. The National Service Act of 1939 did require women to play a part in the railway service, but this was mainly in assisting the evacuation of children rather than carrying out railway work. This took various forms. Women could volunteer to travel with children being evacuated, try to find accommodation for children where householders had spare rooms, or even look after children in large reception centres when homes could not be found for them. There was also the option of taking in evacuees themselves, a role that was paid at the rate of ten shillings and sixpence per week for the first child, and eight shillings and sixpence for any others.

The 1939 Act also asked men with certain railway experience, or those with other transport experience, to enlist for the army's Supplementary

Reserve. There were three sections of this – A, B and C – and it was section A, the transportation and docks unit, that was looking for those with railway experience.

Railways had always attracted a lot of attention from enthusiasts, and taking photographs of trains was a regular pastime for those with an interest. As soon as the war began, anyone taking photographs or even carrying a camera in the wrong place came under suspicion. This was a pity because so many old and unusual locomotives that would normally have been scrapped were still in use due to the war. These would have been of real interest to those who liked to have a photographic record of the trains they had seen, as would with the new Austerity and American engines that were to make an appearance.

The importance of the railway system to the war effort was quite obvious in 1939. It is easy to forget that the road system in the country at the time was nowhere near as modern as the railways. At the outbreak of war, cars were still relatively rare amongst the public and the road system had not been developed to any great extent. In many rural areas, the roads were still more suited to horse-drawn transport, the use of which was still widespread.

The railway system in Britain was a different matter. It was the most modern in the world, with more than 37,000 miles of track, and the

19. An engine at sheds at Plaistow. The line through the station was once owned by the LMS but later became part of the District Line. There were works and engine sheds next to the station until before the war.

20. A train heading towards Shoeburyness, which was an experimental artillery site with its own railway system for many years and was in use throughout the war as a coastal gunnery school.

Mallard had just set the world speed record for a steam-driven locomotive. New engines were still being made up to the beginning of the war, and they were more streamlined and modern than those they replaced. The railway system was perhaps better prepared for the war than either the British government or the armed forces.

This could well have been the reason that, in 1938, Ernest Lemon, railway engineer and Vice President of the London Midland and Scottish Railway, was appointed to be Director-General of Aircraft Production for the Air Ministry, which at the time had been months behind production targets, resulting in the only aircraft that Britain had to defend itself becoming almost obsolete.

Ernest Lemon, the son of a labourer, had begun aged 14 as an apprentice at a railway works and by 1931 had risen to become Vice President of Operating and Commercial of the LMS. He had used the principles of Scientific Management and applied them to all areas of the LMS. He went on to apply the same methods to aircraft production, resulting in amazing improvements that gave Britain enough modern aircraft to fight the Luftwaffe.

Although the bombing of Britain by the Germans was anticipated once war had broken out, there had already been bomb attacks in the country. From 1939 to 1940, the Irish Republican Army (IRA) carried out a sabotage campaign against the infrastructure of the United Kingdom to demonstrate their refusal to accept the legitimacy of the Irish partition. This involved threats to and actual attacks on public services and structures such as power stations and electricity pylons, banks, hotels, shops, cinemas, museums, royal palaces and government buildings. All transport systems and their locations were vulnerable. The railways were first targetted in February 1939, when bombs exploded in the London Underground stations of Tottenham Court Road and Leicester Square, and also at King's Cross station. As the campaign continued, bombs exploded at Midlands railway stations at Coventry, Nottingham, Leicester, Warwick, Derby, Birmingham and Stafford, and again in London, at Victoria and King's Cross stations. The bombing campaign caused some fatalities and many injuries.

In a tear gas attack on two Liverpool cinemas on 5 May 1939, a man was seen to let something fall from his coat. There was then a loud explosion. Crowds leaving one of the cinemas chased the man, who was apprehended by a railway policeman, a demonstration of how railway staff were already on the alert and prepared for attacks before the German bombing began.

* * *

Despite the danger from the IRA and the threat of imminent war, Manchester was described as calm but active as the end of August 1939 approached. There was an unusual activity going on as children were asked to attend school on Saturday for evacuation practice. Although the railways weren't involved in the practices, some groups walked to their local station in anticipation that they may have to be evacuated by train. The railways had, nevertheless, been training for gas attacks and air raids.

The evacuation of children, the elderly and pregnant women from areas at risk of bombing was one of the first major tasks of the railways.

DEFENCE REGULATIONS

IMPORTANT ANNOUNCEMENT

BILLETING

The Government have announced that the dispersal of people in priority classes from certain large towns shall be put into effect immediately.

The area covered by the..Council is a reception area* to which some of these people are being brought.

Occupiers of housing property in this area are required by law to provide accommodation for any persons assigned to them by the Billeting Officer. Every effort will be made to spread the burden of billeting fairly and equally between households.

It may be necessary to carry out billeting at night as well as day-time. Your co-operation in this emergency is requested.

An allowance will be paid to occupiers for the accommodation provided. To claim this you will need a billeting allowance order form. Watch the bottom of this notice for further information about how to obtain the form.

CLERK OF THE COUNCIL

*If only part of the area is scheduled as a reception area, the districts affected are shown below:

Instructions for obtaining billeting allowance order form:

21. A government information form, which makes it clear that accepting displaced persons into your home was not always a voluntary process during evacuation.

This began in September 1939, having been planned many months before. It was anticipated that there would be up to 3 million evacuees. The real number was to be less than 1 million. Often, when hundreds of evacuees were expected to arrive at railway stations, only a handful would turn up. At other stations, where none were expected, hundreds arrived.

The government had decided that evacuation would begin on 1 September, despite the fact that Britain was not yet at war. The announcement had been broadcast a number of times by the Secretary of State for Scotland, John Colville, and the Minister for Health, Walter Elliot. The government stated that no one should conclude that this decision meant that war was inevitable.

The scheme applied to schoolchildren, younger children accompanied by their mother or a responsible person, expectant mothers, the blind and cripples. Schools in the affected areas were closed for the day to allow for the evacuation to take place but those in reception areas were to be kept open for the arrivals.

The evacuation areas were listed in the press and involved most of London and its surrounding areas, as far east as Northfleet and as far west as Acton. The Medway towns were also included, as were coastal areas such as Portsmouth, as well as Liverpool, Manchester, Birmingham, Sheffield and Newcastle, among others. Children to be evacuated were to be sent to school with hand luggage containing a gas mask, a change of underwear, nightclothes and toiletries. They were also to carry enough food for the day.

In Scotland, the categories were the same, as were the instructions for evacuees. The areas affected there were Edinburgh, Glasgow, Dundee, Clydebank and Rosyth. Children who lived in the less populated areas of these towns and cities were not required to be evacuated, although their parents could send them if they wanted to.

The public were asked not to travel unless absolutely necessary, so that evacuation could take place. There was to be a normal railway service before 8.00 am and after 5.30 pm, with the evacuation taking place between these times. The Southern were to run all their normal early business trains into London, which would then be used as evacuation trains. The LPTB issued the same warnings that from 9.00 am until 6.00 pm, rail services for ordinary passengers would be severely curtailed.

In Manchester, Victoria station was the principal point of departure for evacuees, and there were thousands of children all heading for different places. They had been bussed to reception points at the station car park near Todd Street, the Great Ducie Street entrance and the entrance in Bridge Street. The children were separated into groups of ten, each with a teacher or volunteer in charge. School doctors and nurses also travelled to the reception areas.

More than 50,000 people were moved from Manchester on the first day of evacuation. These were mostly children, of course, but the total included 2,000 teachers and 3,500 helpers. It took 114 trains and 150 buses, and led to the closing of 286 schools.

22. Children were often evacuated in school groups. These members of the Boys' Brigade are possibly being evacuated together, although they, as well as Boy Scouts, still attended group camps during the war.

The most common belief when it comes to the evacuation of children was that they went to stay with families in reception areas. In most cases, this was true, but there has been less publicity about the special camps that were built to house children. The National Camps Corporation was a government scheme begun in 1939. The camps were originally built as educational holiday centres but quickly became camps for evacuees in wartime. Some schools moved as a group to these camps along with their teachers. The original plan was for fifty camps but only thirty-one opened in England and five in Scotland.

The evacuation was not well organised by the government. It was frequently left to the staff at railway stations to sort out the mess. At times, the evacuees would be sent out on the first train available, which often led to chaos at the arrival point. When trains with no corridors were used, it meant that young children had no access to toilets and led to unscheduled stops at stations.

In addition to the evacuation of children from their homes, many patients were also moved from London hospitals to free up spaces for expected air raid victims. There were also plans to move the majority of

23. Evacuees leaving Yarmouth station. Some coastal areas became reception points for early evacuees but were then also evacuated as the danger of invasion grew. (*Gillian Mawson*)

people away from coastal areas in Kent, but this didn't materialise at this time.

The main railway termini in London could not cope with the numbers so many evacuees were taken by road or train to other stations such as Richmond, Wimbledon and New Cross Gate. It was the greatest civilian movement ever undertaken by the railway system, with up to seventy-five trains a day taking evacuees from London. Most of the evacuees went to Kent and Sussex.

When Terry Heather was evacuated from Dagenham, large numbers of children from his school were taken by bus to the local railway station. Terry was sent to Somerset and his only memory of the train journey was of a man with an accordion at the end of the carriage playing *Wish Me Luck as You Wave Me Goodbye*. It is very hard to imagine how these children must have felt being sent away from their parents with paper labels attached to them like parcels, or how the parents themselves felt. When Gertrude Walker's husband went off to fight, her two older children were evacuated with their school, while Gertrude, who was pregnant, and her youngest child were evacuated together but not with the older children.

Evacuees had varied experiences. Some remember their parents taking them to the station, unaware that they would not be accompanying them until the train left and their parents were still on the platform. Others remember their parents not even being allowed to come to the station to see them off.

When Christine Jones from Peckham was evacuated, she remembered having one case and a gas mask in a cardboard box. As the war went on, many of the children decorated the boxes they carried. The train Christine travelled on had no toilets but they stopped at a few stations on the way to allow for toilet breaks. There were enough seats for them all, but there wasn't any food on the train, and in many cases the children's parents hadn't thought to send any with them.

Christine and the other children expected to be evacuated for a few months at the most. They didn't expect the war to last so long. The 500 children from her school, along with their teachers and the headmistress, arrived at Charing in Kent. The people waiting to take them in had been told to expect junior-aged children but found themselves getting senior schoolchildren.

The evacuation of vulnerable people took place while the railways were carrying increased amounts of freight and transporting the British Expeditionary Force. Also at this time, many of the warehouses at London's docks were being emptied and the goods carried to safer destinations by train. The contents of many of London's museums and art galleries were also being moved.

It is hard to blame the government for the chaos that evacuation caused. The idea that travel on railways should be restricted to priorities of military use was severely curtailed by the numbers of evacuees travelling. When the expected bombing didn't materialise, many of the evacuees travelled home again, thus intensifying the pressure on the railways. When the bombing did begin, those children who had returned were again evacuated by train. Terry Heather was one of those who returned to Dagenham after a month or so away, only to be sent away again when the bombing started.

24. An interesting wartime advertisement in that, unlike other railway advertisements of the time, it mentions British Railways and not the Big Four or the Railway Executive Committee.

The rapid and efficient DISTRIBUTION of the NATION'S ESSENTIAL SUPPLIES depends upon the smooth running of 1,250,000 FREIGHT VEHICLES worked by BRITISH RAILWAYS

BRITISH RAILWAYS ARE CARRYING ON

In the following days, there was more bad news for London travellers when a number of Underground stations were closed. The public were told that 'certain works' made it necessary to close many stations until further notice. There were nearly twenty stations closed, which included the Underground parts of mainline stations such as King's Cross and Waterloo.

The reason why some of the stations were closed was not revealed until the following month, when it was announced that some of the stations were having sliding doors fitted to prevent flooding if a bomb was to be dropped close enough to the Thames to allow river water to enter the tunnels. The doors would close during an air raid and no trains would enter the tunnels involved.

As with other events during the war, legends about the evacuation developed. There was a story about a mother who put her baby on a train and went to get a cup of tea, returning to find that the train had gone without her. The mother was then sent on an express to Basingstoke, which was faster than the train in which the baby was travelling. Arriving at her destination, the mother found that the baby had been taken off at Clapham Junction and returned to the original point of departure.

The actual numbers of children, parents and teachers who were evacuated in 1939 was 1,334,358. Of these, 600,000 came from the London region and the rest from other major industrial areas, Manchester being the second largest to London. As traumatic as evacuation may have been for the railways, they were to face even more difficult movement challenges as the war progressed, often without the preparation time they had had for evacuation.

There appears to have been some panic involved in the early evacuation. No one really knew what the effects of widespread bombing would be on places like London. Many estimates of the potential extent of death and damage were based on the experiences of the Spanish Civil War. This was, of course, a totally different situation; London had a much higher level of defence and a better system for dealing with casualties.

The first evacuation was probably one of the greatest controlled movements of people within a very short time that had ever happened. The LMS had a great part to play in this. There were fifteen of their stations involved and they ran 1,450 special trains to carry evacuees. Within four days, they had carried over a half a million passengers, including their normal traffic. The company's electric trains worked on a relay system, carrying evacuees to mainline stations.

It wasn't only British children who were part of the evacuation. German Jewish children who had been brought to Britain as part of the Kindertransport scheme and had been settled in London found themselves evacuated once again, which must have been a stern test after the trauma of having left their own country and their parents so recently. Some of them had only just arrived from Germany.

The images of children arriving at railway stations with a gas mask and a label attached to them is one that often springs to mind when evacuation is mentioned, but this doesn't tell the whole story. Many members of the public had already evacuated themselves from areas such as London. So had a number of government departments, boarding schools, hospitals and foreign nationals. Americans were travelling across to Ireland to make their way home and escape the war. The Bank of England needed two whole trains to carry its staff and documents to a safer location.

Not all of those travelling were fleeing from danger from the enemy. One of the parties that the LMS had to move comprised the Italian Embassy staff and a number of other Italians. Migratory workers from Italy had been settling in Britain since the mid-nineteenth century, with a large concentration of migrants and their descendants located in Scotland by the time of the Second World War. When Mussolini declared war on Britain and France on 10 June 1940, they immediately became the 'enemy within' and were being transported to internment camps in various locations across Britain.

There was early praise of railway workers on the Southern Railway from the General Manager, Mr Gilbert Szlumper, who was also a member of the Railway Executive Committee. He said that he was proud to be their leader because of the magnificent way they had dealt with Air Raid Precautions (ARP) schemes and evacuation. He told the staff to stay cheerful and as fit and well-nourished as they could.

*   *   *

Away from the railway lines there was more to railway engineering than just a move towards production of military hardware in their workshops. As early as 1937, the War Office had asked the LMS not to just make a tank, but to design it as well. The pilot A14 medium tank was built at Crewe. Before it had even been finished, the War Office decided that it wanted a lighter, cheaper vehicle.

The LMS then developed another tank, which was known as the Covenanter, and under the Ministry of Supply co-ordinated the production of 1,771 of these tanks by various companies, although 161 of them were produced at Crewe. However, the tank was found to be unsuitable for use abroad and was mainly supplied to home defence units.

There was further support for the home defence units by the LMS. They converted tradesmen's vans into armoured vehicles armed with a

"ARMAMENTS FIRST." Faster and faster hum the war factory machines. Faster and faster the raw materials reach them. Faster and ever faster the finished products are taken away by British Railways. And it is because British Railways are the life-lines between Factories and Fighting forces that passenger trains are fewer and slower. Until the war is won British Railways' slogan must be "Armaments First."

BRITISH RAILWAYS
G W R   L M S   L N E R   S R

25. A wartime advertisement stating that armaments come first. Like the previous advertisement, it mentions British Railways, but *does* list the Big Four.

Lewis gun. These were known as Armadillos. Instead of competing for materials such as steel, which was needed for other armoured vehicles, the Armadillo was made with two layers of wood with gravel in-between instead of metal armour.

At LMS's Horwich works, three other types of tanks were built – A13 Cruisers, Matildas and Centaurs – and they also produced spare parts for them. These were more successful than the Covenanter, and the A13 Cruiser was used in both Europe and Africa.

Other construction tasks given by the government to the railway companies included ambulance trains. These were being manufactured by seven different railway workshops so they would be available in locations across the country. Each train had cars for doctors and nurses.

The use of hospital trains was not a new concept. They had been used in the First World War but had their origins in a much earlier time. The Grand Junction Railways had, as early 1837, a compartment in the mail van that could be converted to hold a bed for someone who was ill. There was a truck kept at Charing Cross that could carry a road ambulance if needed and by the outbreak of war, all the Big Four had a number of vehicles containing beds and all the necessities of the sick room.

As well as ambulance trains, a similar development saw the provision of evacuation trains. These were to be used to remove casualties from places of danger to areas that were safer. Their design was based on government estimates that air raid casualties would be much higher than they actually were. The trains were mainly used to move patients from city hospitals to those in rural locations, or as substitutes for ambulance trains, rather than for their original use.

The first round of evacuation also coincided with the movement of the British Expeditionary Force down to the south coast and across to France. Moving a large number of troops while also arranging to evacuate so many children put an extra strain on the railway system at a time when they were also taking more responsibility for moving goods. Much of the work was concentrated in the southern part of the country.

26. A Gloucester Wagon Company brake van. Brake vans were used for freight trains, which had no continuous brake system. The only brakes were in the loco and the brake van. Their use continued long after the war ended.

Plans for moving a large force of British soldiers to France had been in place for some time, in fact, since the end of the First World War. There had been several amendments to the plans but they were revised once again by the War Office just a few weeks before the movement took place. The first 100,000 men were carried from various points across the country, from as far away as Scotland down to Southampton, often passing across three different railway companies to reach their objective. The amount of stores, weapons and ammunition that accompanied them was colossal, but unlike in the First World War, there were not many horses.

A train carrying troops that began its journey on the LNER would transport them in the same coaches to their destination. The engine would be replaced as the train reached the area of the next rail company, as would be the driver, fireman and guard. The coaches might then not return to their original rail company for months afterwards.

The movement of special trains such as those carrying troops could cause severe disruption to the normal flow of rail traffic. Regular trains could be ordered to move on to slow lines to allow a special to move through. This would then disrupt traffic already on the slow line. In peacetime, there was enough time to plot this carefully, but during the

27. Southampton Docks played a huge part in the war while owned by Southern Railways. The port was used to send troops abroad and bring them back at various times. This led to Southampton being one of the heaviest bombed areas in the country.

war, these changes were often arranged very quickly and schedules could be further disrupted by a series of specials. Getting there was only part of the problem. Arriving at Southampton, each train had to be emptied or unloaded before the next could get in.

Once that was done, there was another problem, and that was how to get the empty coaches and wagons back to where they were needed. Passenger coaches were not as big a problem as freight wagons. Although most goods wagons could carry a variety of cargo, there were some specialised wagons, and these could cause the biggest problems. In a military objective, trucks able to carry tanks or large guns would have to

28. A pre-war advertisement for Southampton Docks as owned by the Southern Railway. It was a vital part of the company's freight and passenger services.

be returned to the places where they were needed, such as where the guns and tanks were made.

As well as the fear of air raids there was also panic about infiltration by fifth columnists and German paratroopers. This led to guards being sent to railway junctions, tunnels and bridges. It was never a good use of fighting men and as the war went on, these duties were taken over by the Home Guard.

Although war was not declared until September 1939, preparations had begun much earlier. As early as January 1938, rail passengers travelling out of London towards Essex had been surprised to see bright yellow carriages parked in the sidings at Barking. These were Mobile Air Raid Precautions instruction units. The railway companies were adding them to their rolling stock. When war did break out, stationmasters were to be responsible for the safety of their passengers and protecting them from bombing, gas and poison. The new units were to be used to train railway staff.

It was hardly surprising that the threat of gas was uppermost in the minds of the government and the public. It had been widely used in the First World War, with devastating effects on its victims. Training in anti-gas work had begun as early as four years before the war and gas masks were available to the public two years later. Some railway companies encouraged their employees to carry a gas mask when on duty from 1937.

Although the use of gas didn't materialise, the gas safety conditions existed up to the final days of the war. The use of flying bombs by the enemy, even when their defeat looked inevitable, must have made everyone wonder if they would be on the receiving end of a revenge gas attack. The V2 was developed as a 'retribution weapon' for the Allied bombings against German cities.

Keeping the railways running was obviously seen as very important and so railway staff were amongst the first to be supplied with gas masks and steel helmets. Signalmen had their steel cupboards, which became known as Tin Coffins, in which they could hide when bombing began to protect them from flying glass. The signal boxes' large glass windows could be shattered by bombs dropping some distance away.

One of the first measures employed to keep people safe from bombing was the blackout. It was difficult to apply this to railways. Many train carriage windows were painted over, or those with blinds were painted at the edges where the blinds had gaps. Carriage light bulbs were replaced with those of low wattage. An added problem was that the glow from the firebox on steam engines was often visible at night. Canvas covers were designed that stretched from the tender across to the cab to try to block this out. There were so many different types of engines that forty-five different covers were needed for the GWR alone. They were not popular as they reduced visibility, especially after loco windows were painted or

29. There were a number of large railway equipment centres in the country before the war. This image shows a sleeper store at Hayes. Once the war began, the equipment was moved to more numerous, smaller stores to try to keep vital supplies safe from bombing.

covered with plates. The rules concerning covers were later changed so that they had to be in place on top of the engine but the sides could be laced up, giving more ventilation and a better view. The sides only had to be pulled down during a raid. Also, railway goods yards were dangerous places even in daylight hours; during a blackout, they could prove lethal.

The Southern Railway was arguably to suffer the most out of the Big Four during the conflict. This was because it covered the south of the

30. A memorial at Victoria station to the named men from the South Eastern & Chatham Railway Company who died in the First World War. The plaque at the bottom mentions the men from the Southern who died in the Second World War, but does not list names.

31. A second memorial at Victoria station naming the men of the London, Brighton & South Coast Railway who died in the First World War. Again, the men of the Southern Railway who died in the Second World War are mentioned at the bottom of the plaque but are not individually named.

country and was potentially more vulnerable to bombing and the chance of invasion. Much of the Southern's area along the south coast was also in range of shelling from the French coast after France was occupied by the Germans.

The Southern's headquarters, which had been at Waterloo, was moved to the Deepdene Hotel at Dorking, Surrey. The area was obviously much less likely to be bombed than Waterloo. Once the new headquarters had been established, it was discovered that there were caves in the grounds. These were then used to house a control room, meeting room and switchboard, giving the benefit of even greater protection from attack.

Mary Williams came from a railway family. Her grandfather had been a stationmaster and her father was the stationmaster at Bracknell station. Along with her brothers and sisters, Mary also went to work for Southern Railway before the war began. She said that coming from a railway family did not guarantee a job but it did help. She joined the company at 17 and used the railway system to travel from her home in Bracknell to London Bridge, where she worked. A few months later, her job moved to Waterloo, where she was a typist. Just before the war began she was one of the staff who moved to Dorking. Part of her job was to organise special trains for evacuees, as well as for troops on their way to France. She recalled that regular trains were cancelled to make way for the specials and her workload was increased.

Although she was safe in Dorking from the bombing, when it began she would go up on to the hills in the area and watch the attacks on London. She remembered that the majority of the men working on the railway were aged from 30 to 40, as most of the younger men had gone to join the forces. Working for the railway gave Mary some privileges as she was allowed to go to coastal areas such as Southampton, where she had a friend, while members of the public were banned from travelling there.

* * *

Southampton Docks was owned by the Southern Railway and it was mainly from here that members of the British Expeditionary Force were carried across to France at the outbreak of war. The docks were to play a large part in the war, especially after most of the company's work was transferred there after the government took over the docks at Dover.

Docks were prime targets for invasion. Because of this, plans were drawn up so that on the orders of the military, the docks could be immobilised. Cranes, dock gates and other machinery would be rendered useless by the removal of small parts. Railway bridges over rivers would also be disabled.

During the early stages of the war, there was often confusion on the railways as it wasn't always clear what was going on. In one instance, a Cheltenham Race Course excursion train set off from Paddington, at a time when most excursions had been cancelled. This train should have been cancelled as the race meeting had been called off anyway. It was stopped at Slough and returned to Paddington, where the passengers were refunded their fares.

Towards the end of 1939, after the early rush of evacuees and the main portion of the BEF had been successfully moved, a further task was imposed on the railways, but on this occasion, there wasn't any time to prepare for it. As well as British soldiers being mobilised to defend the country, troops were being raised throughout the empire. When the first Canadian troops arrived at Liverpool in November, they then had to be moved on to their final destinations.

Without having had advance warnings of the arrivals, the railways began to devise standard pathways along which troops could be moved by large numbers of special trains. This would, in theory, create as little disturbance to other services as possible. Orders from the War Office could be sudden and sent to several rail districts at once, and when this happened, they implemented prearranged plans for holding back other traffic.

Also in November, there was an initiative to help parents see their evacuated children. Special arrangements were made for cheap railway tickets for this purpose. The excursions would be run on Sundays, at monthly intervals, to reception areas. These would only cover travel to areas where cheap fares were not already available. They also only applied to journeys that could be made there and back in one day. For a ticket to a destination 100 miles away, the cost was eleven shillings; a ticket to a destination 160 miles away would cost twelve shillings and sixpence. Parents of children who were ill were given free tickets.

Logistical problems occurred again in December, when up to 1,000 men a day would arrive at Southampton from France on leave. The issue was that all the men wanted to get home, and their homes could be anywhere in the country. The only solution was for the Southern Railway to run two specials a day to London. From there, the men could use the passenger services to get home. This did not help those based in distant or remote locations as they then faced long and difficult forward journeys.

The Southern had a great deal of experience in carrying passengers from the coast to London. Before the war, the company had developed a new class of locomotive. This was the Merchant Navy class, which

BRITISH RAILWAY DOCKS
AND HARBOURS
SERVING THE NATION

The important Docks and Harbours owned by the British Railway Companies are giving invaluable service to the Nation, by means of their facilities for discharging and loading all types of cargoes, and are thus contributing effectively to the National needs. The principal Docks owned by the British Railway Companies are :—

ENGLAND & WALES

BARROW-IN-FURNESS	HULL
BARRY	IMMINGHAM
CARDIFF	MIDDLESBROUGH
FLEETWOOD	NEWHAVEN
FISHGUARD	NEWPORT
FOLKESTONE	PORT TALBOT
GARSTON	PLYMOUTH
GRIMSBY	SOUTHAMPTON
HEYSHAM	SWANSEA
HOLYHEAD	THE HARTLEPOOLS

SCOTLAND

ALLOA	GRANGEMOUTH
AYR	METHIL
BONESS	STRANRAER
BURNTISLAND	TROON

BRITISH RAILWAYS
THE WORLD'S LARGEST DOCK OWNERS

32. A list of the docks owned by the railways in England, Scotland and Wales during the war. They are described as belonging to British Railways, not the Big Four.

had been built to replace the Lord Nelson class on the Channel ferry trains. The weight of Continental sleepers had been too much for the Lord Nelsons. After the outbreak of war, the ferry trains were no longer needed so the Merchant Navy locomotives were transferred to the heavy trains on the Salisbury to Exeter line.

One of the biggest changes in relation to the docks owned by the railway companies came about because of a decision made by the Railway Executive Committee. The east coast was closest to the enemy and was at the greatest danger from their aircraft, shipping and submarines. The ideal would have been to transfer shipping from all eastern ports to the west. There were even plans to move cranes across the country from the unused ports.

Places like Harwich, which had been an important trade centre with Europe, became a naval base instead. The LNER's marine repair shop there was converted to a naval repair base; the railway company no longer had much use for their ships and boats as they had mostly been taken over by the Admiralty.

The plan to move everything to the west did not happen as expected. In the early part of the conflict, many of the eastern ports continued to

33. The SS *St Helier* was built by John Brown in 1925 for the GWR. It serviced the Channel Island routes. In 1939, it became a troopship and then did several trips across the Channel during the Dunkirk evacuation.

be used to carry supplies across to the British Army in France. Many of the wounded returning from Europe also landed on the east coast. Throughout the war, ships were sailing into the Thames to the London docks. Ships were still being built at Hull, and iron and steel was arriving there. As the war progressed, the ports on the east coast became less well used while those on the west coast were busier.

The changes led to a shift in rail traffic as the old systems of carrying goods from the declining ports tailed off. The eastern coast had also been the route for ships carrying coal from the north to the south of the country. As the Admiralty requisitioned greater numbers of vessels, the movement of coal became more landlocked and added an extra strain to the railway system.

The expected bombing had not begun by the end of 1939, but there was some damage to the tracks and injury to servicemen when three trains collided at Selby, North Yorkshire. A statement from the LNER said that three coaches of the passenger train from Doncaster to York had become derailed just north of Selby. An express from King's Cross stopped at signals but was then run into by an express from Leeds to Hull. Three soldiers on forty-eight-hour leave were injured. They were kept in hospital but their injuries were not serious.

34. The *Great Bear* was a Pacific type 4-6-2 built at Swindon in 1908 for the GWR. There were a series of problems and it was converted into a Castle class 4-6-0 and renamed *Viscount Churchill* in 1924.

The end of the year was also to see a large order for locomotives and wagons from the Ministry of Supply. They ordered 240 2-8-0 freight tender engines, 10,000 20-ton covered goods wagons and mechanical handling equipment for docks from the Locomotive Manufacturers Association. The order was worth £9,750,000. The locomotives and wagons were to be used on the French railways by the BEF.

There were a number of railway improvement schemes in place before the war that were put on hold once war began. One of these was the electrification of the line between Manchester and Sheffield. About half the structure was ready to carry the transmission wires. A new steam and electric locomotive depot near Sheffield reached a stage of almost completion.

Another delay in development was on the London Underground, where an extension to the Central Line out to the east was also put on hold – a decision that was to affect a number of people in the later years of the war, some for the better but for many, much for the worse.

Chapter 4

1940

The production of what were known as Austerity locomotives took place throughout the years of the war. They were built using fewer materials than the pre-war types of locos and were made by various engineering companies while many of the railway workshops were doing war work. There were a number of different designs.

The first of the Austerity locomotives were built in 1940. The 2-8-0 locos were designed by Sir William Stanier, Chief Mechanical Engineer of the LMS. The design was adopted by the Ministry of Supply for locomotives for overseas service. When France fell, the engines were lent to the LMS but were later sent to the Middle East. Nos. 300 to 399 were built by the North British Locomotive Company Glasgow; Nos. 400 to 449 were built by Beyer Peacock and Company – all in 1940.

The War Department also took control of some of the older engines from the Big Four. The GWR 0-6-0 Dean locomotives were designed by William Dean in 1883 and made at Swindon. Several of them were taken over by the War Department in the First World War and more than 100 were again used by the War Department in the Second World War. A number of them were lost in France after Dunkirk.

The government were warning the public that one of the areas at risk of sabotage by fifth columnists was the railway. Before the outbreak of the war, instructions had been given to various public bodies about evilly disposed persons who may attempt sabotage. The warnings had been given during the IRA atrocities and were again repeated.

Early in the year, the lack of materials was causing problems for the new blackout lighting systems on trains. It was hoped that the lighting system on London suburban trains would be completed by March. Only a fifth of the British railway accommodation had been adapted to the new form of lighting by this point. There were 42,000 carriages operated by the mainline companies, so it was no easy task.

The new lights included reading lamps, which were switched on when the train was moving and switched off when in a station. This was to stop lights being shown when doors were opened. The passengers were made aware that they had to keep the blinds closed when the lights were on.

The blackout was causing more problems than just those related to lighting. There had been an increase in crime at London railway stations. There had also been some robberies with violence, especially close to Euston. The largest part of the problem was theft from goods yards, which were dimly lit due to the blackout, making it easier for thieves to operate unseen. Pilfering had reached such levels that a special watch was being kept.

The change to the government running the railways didn't make much difference to the staff of the Great Western Railway. The company didn't mention the changes very much to the staff. Even the war hadn't made much difference up to this point. One adjustment that affected older workers was that there had been compulsory retirement at age 60 before the war. This was changed to 61 or at the end of the conflict, whichever came first. Staff could appeal but they were expected to carry on working while their appeal was being processed. There was also

35. Paddington was a busy passenger station but also had a large indoor goods depot, which seems very chaotic in this photograph.

quicker promotion from goods to passenger trains and cleaners could become firemen much more rapidly as the number of staff declined due to enrolment in the forces.

There was an increase in women working on the railways from early in the war but at the GWR, there was not a great deal of effort in recruiting women. When Violet Lee joined as a passenger guard in 1940 at Gloucester, it was made clear to her that the job was for the duration of the conflict and that once the men began to return after the war, her employment would end. It seemed that mechanical engineer Mr C.B. Collett may have had some influence over the lack of pursuing women's enlistment. After his retirement, more women were taken on.

In addition to the wartime stresses imposed on the railways, there was also the problem of bad weather. The winter of 1939/40 was so severe that heavy snow brought down 500 miles of signal and telegraph wires on the GWS system. The weather also caused increased sickness amongst staff and absences were up by a quarter.

In January 1940, there were snowdrifts of 10 to 15 feet deep and more than 300 snow ploughs were working to clear the lines. Some of them were driven by four engines. At one point, there were six passenger and two freight trains stranded on the West Coast Main Line at the same time.

The points froze and on electric lines the conductor rail was often covered in ice. London Transport's system had sleet trains, but they were useless against the thick ice on the rail. Ice had to be chipped off by hand. Some electric trains had to be pulled by steam locomotives, which were in control of the brakes so the driver had to communicate with the electric motorman using hand signals.

At the end of January, services out of Manchester were, at best, patchy. Information on travel conditions was uncertain. An early morning traveller wanting to get to Darwen was told that he could be booked as far as Bolton, where there were believed to be connections to Preston, and from there to Blackburn or Accrington. There was also a tram route from Blackburn to Darwen but the railway officials had no information on whether the trams were running.

Trains to Blackpool from Manchester had not been running for two days but had then been restored using single-line traffic. A serious shortage of milk occurred in Manchester as it could not get there from

36. The Cornish Riviera was served by the GWR and was portrayed as a wonderful holiday destination before the war. The train shown is the Cornish Riviera Express, which no doubt carried many servicemen during the war.

farms in Cheshire and Derbyshire. Supplies of potatoes and meat were also under threat.

* * *

When new staff were employed they needed training, but it wasn't only on the railways that staff were being taught how to drive trains. The Railway Training Centre of the Royal Engineers at Longmoor was also teaching men to become train drivers. There were hundreds of them in training. They would watch the work of skilled drivers and firemen, although many of them had some railway experience as they had come into the forces from railway companies.

The railways could no longer afford to lose even partly trained personnel to the forces as they were so short of men. Therefore, many of the military trainees for railway duty were coming from other occupations. Where a railwayman was found to have joined another branch of the services, they were often transferred to the Royal Engineers.

As well as learning how to drive the trains, men were taught how to construct tracks, make embankments and maintain the stock. The Royal Engineers could at any time be called upon to construct or work on railways in any part of the world and had to have experience of every possible system of signalling and switching. Most of this was learnt on a model railway layout.

The officers and instructors at the training centre were all specialists with many years of experience. The Railway Engineer and Staff Corps was a separate branch of the Royal Engineers, and included amongst its higher ranking officers were men who had been the heads of civilian railways.

Although there may have been co-operation between different groups in the war, there was also some level of disagreement. In February 1940, there was a dispute between the LMS and the users of the company docks. Fleetwood Chamber of Trade had challenged the decision by the LMS to recover from the dock users the cost of providing air raid shelters for them. The government had made it obligatory to provide shelters for all users of the dock and the LMS had decided that it was entitled to make the claim.

37. Heysham Dock was used for ferries to both Ireland and the Isle of Man. There was a large ICI factory nearby, which was a target during the war. The dock was owned by the LMS.

The cost was estimated at £2 to £3 per person. Many of the Fleetwood users complained, and argued that the government Act did not give the LMS the right to charge for the shelters. The LMS then attempted to get a supplementary order to authorise them to reclaim the cost.

In May, the Ministry of Supply made an inspection of the locomotives and wagons being constructed for the BEF. They were assessing the completed items at locomotives works in the Midlands, which although not named in the inspection report, was, I believe, Bayer Peacock. At one of these inspections, a train was presented to a M Leguille of the French National Railways. It was a French type train with 20-ton covered wagons, and was the first of the thousands ordered for use in France.

The wagons were wider than those used on British railways and the doors had to be taken off for their journey to the ports. As well as the goods being made for France, the company was also making steel coaches for the London Underground, while also manufacturing other rolling stock for South Africa and Egypt. Of course, no one was to know that the locomotives and trucks being made for France were not going to get there as within weeks of the inspection and the handing over of the train, the BEF were on their way back to Britain.

Coal was presenting another problem. Before the war, each railway company had made their own arrangements with colliers. Now there were limits set by the Ministry of Fuel and coal that had previously been imported was no longer available, so the companies now had to share resources.

It wasn't only coal that was in short supply. There was also a move towards salvaging items that might previously have been thrown away. A film, *Saving our Scrap*, was shown all over the south of the country. All old rails, pipes, iron and steel was to be reused. Paper was also saved and bins were placed on stations to collect it from the public.

There was to be a closer wartime relationship between the railway

38. Coal was a vital resource in the war and its importance was even broadcast on the labels of matchboxes.

system and the military. There had already been a lot of troop movement taking men to the Channel ports to reach France. The need to move troops in the event of an invasion was now paramount. There was creation of a new role, that of Railway Liaison Officer, who would deal with the military.

A big event for the London, Midland and Scottish Railway in 1940 saw Ernest Lemon returning to the company from the Air Ministry. It wasn't the return that he had been expecting, however, considering all he had done for them before he left. He felt as though he wasn't welcome and was given a number of jobs that didn't match his abilities. Perhaps this was because they had managed without him.

As well as Lemon not feeling welcome, he was also affected by the departure from the company of Tommy Hornbuckle, who had been the manager of the Chief Mechanical Engineering Department at Derby and had once been Lemon's ally. He was also his brother-in-law, having married Lemon's wife's sister, although this was not common knowledge.

Even though they may previously have been allies, there were some problems between them on Lemon's return. These may have been personal as Lemon had split up with his wife, putting Hornbuckle in an awkward position. It has also been suggested that they were in competition with each other and that Hornbuckle was not happy because the company seemed to have little interest in moving towards diesel trains, which he was in favour of, apart from those used for shunting.

Lemon eventually got his old job back but there had been changes at the company. Now all decisions were made by the Railway Executive Committee. There was little room for development or the construction of new rolling stock. All raw materials had been allocated for military use and the Derby works were almost completely engaged in aircraft construction and repair.

*   *   *

May 1940 was to herald one of the darkest times of the war for Britain. On the 13th of the month, men and freight were still being carried across to France from Southampton Docks. Four days later, all the ports were closed. On 26 May, Operation Dynamo began and the main job of carrying the British troops back home fell to Southampton.

The first moves in the evacuation of the British Army from France were kept secret. There was a meeting between the Railway Executive Committee and the Big Four. The Southern Railway Superintendent of Operations suggested to the military authorities that secrecy might cause more of a problem than publicising the event. At one GWR station, the stationmaster was woken up at home at midnight by the police and told to open his station. When he arrived he found three army officers, who swore him to secrecy before telling him about Operation Dynamo.

It would have been very difficult to have kept the movement of so many men secret and, as it happened, the knowledge that was made open to the public was to be a great help as volunteers gathered along the routes to help feed and care for the men as they arrived back into the country over the nine days of the operation.

Not only were Southern's docks and trains used but also the boats that they owned, along with ships owned by the other railway companies At the outbreak of war there were 130 ships owned by the railway companies, most of which had been taken over by the Admiralty.

The company ships included those capable of carrying trains. The Dover-Dunkirk route was operated by three large train ferries able to

39. The SS *Isle of Guernsey* was built in 1930 by Denny and Brothers for Southern Railway's route to the Channel Islands from Southampton. In 1939, she carried RAF personnel to France before becoming a hospital ship that took part in the Dunkirk evacuation. Later, she became a landing ship with six landing craft, carrying Canadian troops on D-Day.

accommodate twelve full-size coaches or forty goods wagons. The three were named after old ferries on the Thames: *Hampton Ferry*, *Twickenham Ferry* and *Shepperton Ferry*. The Southern ships also served the Isle of Wight and the Channel Islands.

The LNER operated ferry services from Harwich to the Hook of Holland, Antwerp and Zeebrugge. On the west coast, the LMS operated ferries between Holyhead and Kingstown, Heysham and Belfast, and Liverpool and Belfast. The company also ran cargo boats to Ireland.

Of the forty-two craft owned by the Southern company, twelve were lost during the Dunkirk evacuation. This included a hospital ship, *Paris*, which came under aerial attack on 2 June while trying to rescue another hospital ship, the *Worthing*. It was well known that women later played a large part in running the railways during the war but as early on as this, one lady, previously a carriage cleaner at Brighton, had been operating as a stewardess on the *Paris*. Mrs Lee was thrown into the water during the attack and was in the midst of machine-gun fire. She was picked up by a lifeboat, but that too came under attack and she found herself back in the water, where she remained for an hour and a half before being picked up by a tug and taken back to Dover.

The *Maid of Orleans* carried more than 5,000 men, including 400 French troops, back home before it was damaged after colliding with HMS *Worcester*. The master, Captain Walker, was awarded the Distinguished Service Cross (DSC). The last Southern craft to come back from Dunkirk was the *Whippingham*, a small paddle steamer, which docked on 4 June.

The Great Western sent their ships to help evacuate the men from the beaches of Dunkirk. Their ferries normally worked between Weymouth and Jersey. There was some discussion about putting naval commanders on the GWR ships but the commanders didn't want that to happen.

Getting the men back across the Channel was, of course, only the beginning. Once back in England they had to be moved again. It was here that the co-operation between the Big Four was so evident. The task of moving the men fell to forty coaches from the Great Western Railway, forty-four from the London and North Eastern Railway, forty from the London Midland and Scottish Railway, and fifty-five from the Southern Railway.

There were trains departing every twenty minutes from Southampton and many didn't know where they were going or where to stop. Many drivers were told to go to Guildford and ask for directions from there. As well as Southampton, men were arriving at Dover, Folkestone, Ramsgate, Sheerness, Newhaven and other south coast ports.

The Southern were used to dealing with large crowds when sporting fixtures took place in their area such as the Epsom Derby, as well as for events in London, but this evacuation was obviously run on a much less organised timetable. One general supposedly said that he wished that the army could operate with as few written instructions as Southern Railway could.

At the heart of the movement of men was Redhill, on the Brighton to London line. The engines were coaled and watered there but it was so busy that at one point they ran out of water. There were 300 tons of ash left there after the troop movement. About 80 per cent of the large engines could not turn at Woking and had to run to the Addlestone Triangle, which was difficult for drivers who did not know the signals.

The GWS special military trains carried the men to Devizes, then by lorry to local army camps. The company ran 800 special trains and

40. Dover was one of the most significant of the south coast ports during the war. Not only was it bombed but it was also shelled from the coast of France. Due to its importance, it was taken over by the Admiralty.

carried 182,808 men. The chairman of the company, Viscount Horne, thanked the staff for their efforts in the GWR magazine in July.

The men on the trains were often fed by volunteers assisting the army. Food was served at Paddock Wood, Headcorn and Tonbridge. At Penge, the Salvation Army band played to welcome the men home. In Kent, there were not enough cups so tea was served in tin cans. The men were then told to throw the cans out of the windows on to the platform so they could be collected and washed.

The evacuation from France was still going on at the end of May but it wasn't only British troops arriving. There were also men from the French and Belgian armies. People living along the railway lines of some southern suburbs could watch train after train carrying military men away from Dover and Southampton.

The stories of the men returning all repeated the merciless way the German aircraft had machine-gunned those trying to escape the conflict, including civilians. A.B. Bradley of Sunderland said that when men were sent ashore from his ship, he witnessed British soldiers wading through water up to their necks. The rescue work was then carried out in a hail of bombs. On the way home, however, the ship's guns brought down a number of Dorniers.

The numbers of men carried away from the southern ports presented a very difficult task for the railways. It is no surprise then that during such an operation not everything was going to work perfectly. David Robertson, MP for Streatham, during a debate in the House of Commons recounted that the railway companies and the army welfare authorities had failed to provide accommodation for thousands of soldiers, sailors and airmen. In northern stations it was possible to see men who had been brought back from France lying on trolleys and waiting room floors. Robertson went on to say that troops had been forced to buy food from the railway companies' own catering departments while the efforts of voluntary organisations ready to supply food at cost price had been ignored; in some stations, voluntary organisations weren't allowed in. The debate continued and Mr Ralph Etherton, MP for Stretford, said that events that had taken place at Manchester London Road station needed a special inquiry.

A spokesman for the railway companies said that social workers who organised all kinds of services for those evacuated had no complaint

41. Memorial at Manchester Piccadilly for those connected with the LMS who died in the war.

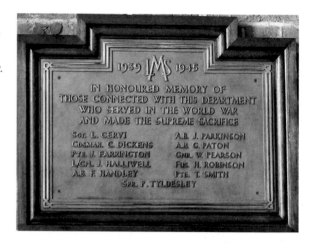

to make. A representative of the YMCA told the *Manchester Guardian* that railway officials at all the stations, including London Road, were most helpful. It was true, though, that only at one station, Manchester Central, were outside agencies allowed to go on to the platforms with refreshments.

Troops travelling into Manchester were well catered for if they had a short time to wait for another train. If they did not have time to leave the station before the next train arrived, they had to take their chances as to whether refreshments were provided. Another YMCA worker said that he had no idea why organisations like his own were not allowed on to the platforms in Manchester when they had been allowed in other northern station like Leeds and Preston. The men arriving at London Road station were only two minutes' walk away from a YMCA hostel, where there were also beds available.

There is little doubt that the railway companies did a tremendous job in getting the thousands of men coming across the Channel away from the south coast. There was a great deal of making do and managing the best they could in such an unusual situation and there was not a perfect outcome for everybody involved, but in such a situation, could there ever be?

Many of those who returned from France with injuries ended up in hospital, and the Red Cross Society and the Order of St John were on hand to distribute railway concession vouchers to the relatives of the sick

42. Soldiers on their way back from Dunkirk being given refreshments by volunteers. These actions were repeated at a number of stations on their various routes. (*Mirrorpix*)

and wounded to allow them to visit their family members. The vouchers were given by the railway companies and entitled the bearer to a return ticket for the price of a single.

Meanwhile, at the same time that the evacuation of the men from Dunkirk was going on there had been a new wave of evacuation from London. Many of those who had returned home after the Phoney War were now beginning to leave London again after the Germans had overrun France. The most intense waves of evacuation, however, were happening in the coastal areas of the south and the east of England, where there was now a greater danger of invasion.

In May 1940, thousands of children were moved from the coasts of Kent, Essex and Suffolk in sixteen special trains. In June, there were a further 48,000 from the east coast on seventy special trains. More than a 100,000 from London were moved to Berkshire, Somerset, Devon and Cornwall in eighty-four special trains. Once again, the main London termini were unable to cope and many evacuees left from Vauxhall, Clapham Junction, Earlsfield and Wimbledon.

There was still very little idea of how many children would take up the offer of evacuation. At Vauxhall there were plans to move 600 children but only 417 turned up. The numbers from London increased again later in the year after the Blitz began in September. The hop pickers of Kent, who had spent the summer on working holidays from London, were unable to go home and were taken to other parts of the country.

Although Operation Dynamo was over by 4 June, the danger of invasion meant that it was important to make sure that as many British troops could be brought back from Europe as possible. Two of the LMS ships, the *Princess Maud* and the *Duke of York*, were sent to Valery-en-Caux on 11 June and came back with 1,700 men who had managed to evade capture. The *Duke of York* had been hit by three shells and her chief officer had picked another one off the deck and thrown it overboard. Over the next two days, the GWR ships *Roebuck*, *Sambur* and *St Helier*, recently patched up from Dunkirk, tried to save the Highland Division from the same place but were driven off by German guns. One of the LNER train ferries from Harwich that had been with them was sunk with the loss of its fourteen-man crew. There were further attempts to

43. The *Tattershall Castle* was built in 1934 by William Grey for the LNER's Humber ferry service. The ship carried soldiers along the Humber during the war and due to fog was one of the first civilian ships to have radar. Now moored on the Thames, she is used as a pub.

pick up men from Cherbourg but these were unsuccessful, although 80,000 men were picked up from Brest and the *St Helier* retrieved 2,500 men from St Malo.

With the last few French ports fallen, it was impossible to defend the Channel Islands. The situation there had been quite relaxed until this time, having still been advertised as a holiday destination in the spring. The islands were then demilitarised when British troops were withdrawn after Dunkirk. This was to have an impact on the railway companies, mainly in relation to the ships they owned and then with the railways on the mainland.

Plans had been drawn up to evacuate much of the civilian population from the islands but there were conflicting opinions on whether they should stay or leave. At the end of June, the Germans began to bomb the islands, which prompted people to make up their minds more quickly. A number of ships took part in the evacuation, including twenty-five that took people from Guernsey alone.

In addition to the railway ships, another branch of the railway service played a part in the evacuation – Jersey Airways, which was owned by the Southern and the Great Western railways. Along with the people, there were also railway assets and records to move. Towards the end of June, 25,000 refugees from the islands arrived at Weymouth. There were 17,000 from Guernsey, 6,000 from Jersey and 2,000 from Alderney. The evacuees then became the concern of the railway system as they were moved around the country.

Because of the bombing, many of the railway staff were still on the islands when the last of the railway ships had to leave for the final time. Despite requests by the railways to attempt another trip, the government declared it too dangerous. The last person who managed to leave Guernsey was a Mr Prince. He had been supervising the loading of three railway boats. One of his colleagues was wounded in the thigh during an air raid. Mr Prince had to see the three boats off himself and was the last man to get on board.

The movement of so many men during Operation Dynamo gave the railway companies experience of transporting many men. Even so, members of the military still encountered problems moving around the country to postings or on leave. There were calls for rooms and canteens

44. Channel Islands evacuees leaving Crewe. (*Courtesy of the Laine family/Gillian Mawson*)

to be provided for soldiers at London railway stations as they often had to wait many hours for trains.

There were suggestions that the government could commandeer hotels that were close to the stations. These could provide bed, bath and sustenance for military personnel. Not only were they waiting hours for trains, but they often had to walk between London stations at night to get their connection when there were no buses or Underground trains running.

Now there was a new threat for the south coast to face: shelling from the coast of France. The Germans were using both fixed and railway guns to shell Dover and other parts of the south coast. The British response was mainly from fixed coastal batteries. The other participants in the war were using railway guns much more widely than Britain was. Britain had employed railway guns in the First World War but by the time of the Second World War, they had mainly fallen out of use.

It was the period after Dunkirk that was to see the war really begin for the people of Britain. German planes were already flying over the mainland, but only for reconnaissance at this point. Nearly everyone who travelled by train in 1940 was to have personal experience of bombing. They either saw bombing or bomb damage to stations, or had to change from trains to buses due to the damage. Everyone suffered some level of delay.

There were also a number of changes as to how the railways operated. It was important that vital stores were kept safe as it wasn't easy to find replacements. Where there had previously been thirty-two large railway supply stores across the country, there were now 120. These were smaller, so if they were hit in a bombing raid the losses would be less significant.

After Dunkirk, a novel use was found for old railway tracks when they were used to form tank traps. Indeed, military adaptation of a variety of railway equipment and premises was common. For instance, at Dover, mines were stored in the Shakespeare and Lydden tunnels, and the port was taken over by the Admiralty.

The first air raid warning occurred over Salisbury while there were four trains in the station. One was full of troops, another contained wounded men from the SS *Lacastria* and a third was an ammunition train full of naval mines. The trains soon moved out of the town.

There had been some isolated bombing of the country from as early as April 1940, when a bomb fell on Wick, near John O'Groats. This was just after the invasion of Norway. Middlesbrough was bombed at the end of May, but it was the beginning of July before there were heavy raids on Hull. There were further raids all over the country but it was only a taste of what was to come.

The probing by the Luftwaffe continued into July and no one was certain when the bombing would begin in earnest or when an invasion might take place. However, the efforts that the railway workers had already made were recognised in August, when medals were given to a number of staff. Mr R. Holland-Martin, Chairman of the Southern Railway, presented the first batch of the new Southern Railway Meritorious Service Medal.

The medal was designed by George Kruger Gray, in silver gilt due to the shortage of gold. It was shaped like a driving wheel with a laurel wreath. Mr Holland-Martin said that they had learnt something of the patience, endurance and courage, and even heroism of the men in the face of great danger who had taken an army to France and brought it back again.

The first eighteen medals were given to men in all branches of the service, at home, in France and in the Channel. They were: A.M. Newbold, general agent of British Railways, Paris; R.G. Gangloff, agent, Calais; M C.A. Ricci, acting agent, Boulogne; H.H. Golding, captain; F.J. Hemphrey, clerk; G. Hunter, berthing master; F.A. Ford and E.A. Roote, dock gatemen; W. Harris and J.H. Winter, porters; G. Mace, able seaman; T. Haslett, chief inspector; G. Elmes, fireman; T. Cooper, head shunter; G. Oak, crane driver; A. Holmes, wood machinist; F.S. Cox, fireman; and E.H. Batchelor, guard.

It was the Southern Railway area that suffered the worst out of all the Big Four railway areas during the conflict. From 24 August 1940 to 10 May 1941, there were 250 raids in 252 days on the Southern district. The damage caused was not always evident to those using the rail system because much of it was repaired quickly. Instant repairs became part of the railman's job. The first raids on London began in September and on the other large industrial cities from then on until the end of the year.

As with the period after Dunkirk, there was a lot of confusion about evacuation. In one incident, a boy of 7 seemed better informed than

45. Bomb damage to London stations and trains was a common event during the war. This image shows an LMS train in a station after an attack.

railway staff. Arriving at Victoria, the boy asked the stationmaster where he caught the train to Launceston. The stationmaster said it was from Waterloo. The boy replied, 'No, it's leaving from here; I've just been sent from Waterloo.' The telephone lines between the two stations had been knocked out by bombing.

The Great Western did their share of evacuation, taking children from Paddington to the West Country. They also suffered damage from enemy attacks. On 20 August, Newton Abbot station was bombed: fourteen died and twenty-nine were injured. The most damage suffered on the company's area was at Paddington, Bristol, Birmingham, Plymouth and their docks in South Wales, at Barry, Cardiff, Newport, Port Talbot and Swansea.

In addition to the air raids, there was also long-range shelling from German guns in France. The place that suffered most from this was Dover. There was a request to the War Cabinet from Rear Admiral Power, suggesting that special aircraft be used for reconnaissance in regard to the shelling at Dover. Sir Wilfrid Freeman, Vice-Chief of the Air Staff, said he was prepared to use fighters as spotter aircraft and would place a Spitfire or a Defiant at their disposal. It was agreed that the spotter aircraft would need an escort.

There were some early attempts at using 9.2-inch railway guns at Dover in response to the shelling from the French coast. There had been two guns of the same kind sent to France with the British Expeditionary Force, but they were never used because there was no ammunition and they were abandoned close to Dunkirk when the troops were evacuated. There were also 12- and 18-inch railway howitzers at Dover.

As well as First World War guns, the artillery also had a First World War commander. Lieutenant Colonel Montagu Cleeve had commanded a railway battery in the Great War and now he took command of four long-range railway guns. Old railway gun mountings were adapted for these. They were deployed with the Royal Marine Siege Regiment in Dover. They were called HMG Gladiator, Sceneshifter and Peacemaker, and were used to return fire on the Germans in France. They were never as effective as fixed guns and their use was soon changed to training.

When the threat of invasion was at its strongest, a Heavy Regiment, Royal Artillery was raised in September and was equipped with more old

46. One of the railway guns based at Dover that was used to return fire on the German guns in France, with its crew posing on the barrel.

First World War railway guns. This included 9.2-inch guns, the same as those left in France. These were used by the 195 Rail Mounted Battery, who were stationed near Ashford in Kent. The men were positioned in a country house at Great Chart, with a regimental sergeant major who used to be a stationmaster on the Hexham to Riccarton Junction line in Roxburghshire.

The 195 Company managed the railway operations of six to eight railway mounted 9.2-inch guns. Two of these were in Essex and four in Kent. There were also some fixed cross-Channel guns. Each of the guns was moved by an ex-GWR Dean Goods class 0-6-0, which spent most of its time in steam waiting, and rarely moved apart from during training.

The fixed cross-Channel guns were based at Martin Mill on the Dover & Deal Railway. The men responsible for them lived in two semi-detached houses. There was little else there apart from the stationmaster's house and a pub. The guns were fired by Royal Marines. Later, there were two 13½-inch railway mounted naval guns delivered to the location as well.

The railway guns would be moved into position on the railway truck and when ready to fire, the ammunition truck would be moved away to a safe distance. The ammunition would be brought back to reload after firing. There would be four shots from each gun in a firing session. After this, the guns would be moved back into the Guston Tunnel.

Dover was protected by a large number of barrage balloons, which were often targets for German pilots who would shoot them down. The cables that had been attached to the balloons would often fall across the railway lines at Martin Mill. When the men working on the engines there tried to move them, they were told to leave them alone by RAF men. On one occasion, one of the engines had to stop because of the cables and was fired on by German aircraft while stationary, but was unharmed.

Not all trains escaped damage. A train at Dover being pulled by a King Arthur, 797 *Sir Blamor de Ganis*, was attacked by an aircraft's cannon. The shells went through the locomotive's firebox. The engine was then repaired at Ashford with patches over the holes and was running again the next day.

During one training exercise, an Artillery colonel travelled on the footplate of the engine that moved the railway guns but was ordered off by the military engine driver. The driver and his fireman were then arrested. The 195 lieutenant came along on a spare engine and showed the colonel a copy of the military railway rule book. Rule fifty-six said that 'enginemen must not allow any person to ride on the engine unless in the execution of his duty'. The men were then released.

There was a difference between the civilian railway rule book and the military one. The military one was a simplified version containing 102 rules, which was about half the size of the civilian one.

Members of the 195 Company often found themselves on other railway related duties, such as shunting at Hythe. They shunted weekend trains that were used to bring soldiers in off Romney Marsh for a weekend in Hythe or Folkestone. They charged a penny a ride but as it was a military train, no one knew what to do with the money.

It wasn't only shelling that the railways had to put up with. The accuracy of the German bombing was not precise if they were aiming at industrial targets. The raids on Hull had never seriously interrupted the railway system or even managed to put the docks out of action, despite some damage. Many of the bombs fell on the town, which was of no military value whatsoever and just caused hardship for the people.

Southampton suffered in a similar way. The attacks may have been aimed at the docks but much of the town suffered the worst effects.

The results of late evening bombing were felt when trains had to stop running due to the raids. It meant that in many cases, workers were not able to get home. To cope with this, the railway companies put on later trains after the all-clear to get workers back home. Unfortunately, not all passengers were aware of the later trains and many were stranded for the night.

Trains were often chased by planes, so there were restrictions on how many trucks could carry explosive material. Early in the war, the number was restricted to five on each train, but this wasn't feasible and it was soon changed to sixty. The speed was also restricted to 40 miles an hour, which meant that they couldn't outrun a plane. Trains carrying explosives were not allowed to pass other trains in a tunnel, and on the GWR they were not allowed in the Severn Tunnel at all.

There was a great deal of danger at Dover for passengers as well as the railway workers. At one point in August, the trains were stopped because passengers were sheltering in a tunnel from the bombing. The shelling also played havoc with the operation of the trains from the port.

47. A train on the Glasgow Underground. Unlike the London Underground, the Glasgow tunnels were not deep enough to provide safe shelters, as was shown in September 1940 when a bomb badly damaged the tunnels near Merkland Street station.

The loco shed at Dover was close to the shore and while the engines were coaling, a man would stand on the stack of coal watching towards the coast of France. When he saw a flash of gunfire, he would shout a warning and the men would run to the shelters before the shell arrived.

Despite the danger, several of the staff at Dover Priory station served right through the war. They were Mrs Clayton in the booking office, Mr Owen, the chief booking clerk, Mr Galloway, the station foreman, and Mr Savage, the ticket collector. The stationmaster was so busy that he often slept in his office, and was awarded the British Empire Medal for his stalwart meeting of the regular emergencies that took place.

The War Cabinet met in August and discussed the cost of the railways. The Cabinet said that the railways had been making around £40 million profit in the years before the war and were running just over that at that time. If they earned another £5.5 million they would keep it. If the profit went above £45.5 million, they would keep half of the total up to £56 million.

Discussion about the railways often came up during meetings of the War Cabinet and in September they discussed the use of the London

48. Dover Priory station, which suffered constant damage from bombing and shelling throughout the war until just after D-Day.

Underground as air raid shelters. The Cabinet were told that in certain parts of London, the public were reluctant to use street shelters. This was due to a number of direct hits by bombs on them. The public preferred to gather in other underground accommodation, including the Tube.

The Minster of Health said that overcrowding in some shelters was endangering health and that inoculation against diphtheria and scarlet fever may be necessary for those in shelters. The Minister of Transport discussed whether the Tube should be used as shelters but said that it was more important to keep the Underground for transport. The Police Commissioner agreed. The public were meanwhile being told to use shelters, of which more were supposedly being built. However, materials for new shelters were not a priority.

It was mentioned that street shelters were not immune to a direct hit but according to the Cabinet, offered the best protection available. Obviously the public did not agree, which was why they kept going down to the Underground when there was a raid, or even to spend the night there, which the government were against and were trying to stop.

49. Despite government attempts to stop the London Underground from being used as air raid shelters, public action eventually forced them to change their minds, as this sign shows.

Railway structures proved useful in another way in the fight against invasion. Many of the signal boxes and stations in remote areas had wide-ranging views, from where invasion attempts might be spotted. The railway outposts were connected with each other and with control rooms, so messages could be quickly passed to alert the authorities of any danger.

The telegraph and telephone lines were, of course, vulnerable to damage during air raids so railwaymen who owned cars or motorcycles were recruited as despatch riders and put on standby. Thankfully, they were not needed in the case of invasion but did at times perform the service during air raids to report damage.

The railways were also supplied with radio sets, which were generally in short supply. A hundred sets were given out – sixteen to the GWR, twenty-two to the SR, thirty to the LNER and thirty-two to the LMS. The radio sets only had a range of 50 miles so to help the network cover the country, half of them were mounted on road or rail vehicles.

A significant challenge to the railways was moving rolling stock from one place to another so that sufficient trucks were available to move goods, especially from docks when ships arrived. At the end of August, the Minister of Transport gave instructions that goods should be conveyed in open wagons if covered wagons or sheets were not available and the shortage was likely to cause congestion at ports.

The sheets used to cover open trucks were made from flax and some of the usual sources for this material were no longer available. The stock of sheets held by the rail companies was not enough to cope with the increased levels of traffic. The instructions would only come into play when a port emergency committee served notice on a railway company that it was necessary in order to clear the port. Trucks would also not be double sheeted as they had been before. There would be no liability to the company for damage to the goods when the order was given.

In the event of invasion, there were plans to evacuate the majority of the civilian population from the coastal areas affected. This did not include essential workers, which in most cases included railway workers. They had to be ready to move military supplies and personnel to the areas where the invasion had taken place.

One of the main threats from the German army was its mechanisation. The British forces were very short of armoured vehicles so it was imperative that what they did have could be moved quickly to where they were needed. However, to get the tanks on and off the trains, ramps were necessary, and they might not be available where the fighting was going on. A clever innovation to remedy this was the use of long bolster wagons built on removable bogies. One end of each wagon could be lowered on to the rails to provide a ramp to allow tanks to get off the train.

Most factories were supplied with raw materials by rail. A busy time for this was during the harvest, when produce needed to be carried to factories for processing. One of these was the sugar beet factory at Allscott, near Wellington. In 1938, new machinery had been installed that had been made in Germany. When the factory was attacked in August, it was thought that this was due to the knowledge the Germans had about the factory and its machinery.

On 23 August, there was a heavy attack on Southampton and the International Cold Storage building was hit. There was damage to the water supply for the fire services and the fire destroyed 2,000 tons of meat and 2,400 tons of butter. The butter melted and blocked the drains and also ran into the sea.

In September, there was so much damage to London stations that the mail trains could not run and the mail was held up. Eventually, it had to

50. Damage to a London station with a train in it. A crane is being used to move wreckage to get the system running again quickly.

be sent by road. The newspapers had the same problem as they travelled through Waterloo, which was at one point closed. The newspapers were then sent by road to Wimbledon, but it was found that the road was blocked. They were then taken to Surbiton. These were common occurrences as no one ever knew what problems they would face each day as they tried to go about their normal routine.

The rapid repair of lines and the co-operation between the services was seen on 8 September, when a bomb fell on the viaduct carrying eight lines between Waterloo and Vauxhall. Three of the lines were left spanning a crater caused by the bomb, which had also destroyed twelve motor vehicles that had been beneath the arch. A unit of Royal Engineers arrived to help repair the lines. They shored up the rails so that two lines could be reopened within twelve hours of the bomb landing. It took a further nine days to get another three lines working, which then relieved the strain on the first two lines. By 1 October, the viaduct had been repaired and all lines were open again.

The start of the Blitz in early September 1940 saw many people in London seeking shelter and the obvious place to find this was in the tunnels of the London Underground. Taking shelter in the Underground was not a new idea. It had been used during the First World War when bombs fell from Zeppelins and, later, aircraft. The level of bombing in the Great War was, of course, nothing like the level it was in the Second World War.

Large numbers of people sheltering in stations caused severe inconvenience to the railways and interrupted the smooth running of the trains. There were attempts to control the number of people using the Underground for shelter although efforts to stop this had as good as ended by this time. The government felt that using the Underground could create a 'shelter mentality', which in some cases it did as some members of the public set up home in stations and other unusual places like the caves in Kent. It soon became evident, however, that the public were going to occupy the tunnels whatever the government said.

The heavy bombing of 7 and 8 September led to the public shelters in London becoming overcrowded. The shelters were unhygienic, which prompted many members of the public to seek refuge in the Underground. On 8 September at Liverpool Street, railway officials and troops tried to stop members of the public sheltering in the station. A large crowd managed to force their way in, resulting in a change in government policy and the opening of the Underground as a shelter.

By the middle of September, shelter marshals were appointed to officially supervise in the Underground and first aid staff and toilets were also provided. Shelter mentality may have affected a few, but generally, the public used the Underground only during heavy raids.

A War Cabinet meeting in October discussed the use of the Underground as shelters and they were obviously coming round to the idea that the people were going to use it. There was

---

AIR RAID SHELTER

PERSONS MAY SHELTER HERE AT THEIR OWN RISK AFTER THE TAKE COVER NOTICE HAS BEEN GIVEN

Persons sheltering are not allowed to take Birds, Dogs, Cats and other Animals, as well as Mailcarts, on to the Company's premises.

BY ORDER.

Electric Railway House,
Broadway, Westminster

51. The notice informs those sheltering in the Underground that they were there at their own risk once the all-clear was sounded, and they were not allowed to bring pets with them.

---

an argument that because raids were quite short, there was no need to provide elaborate amenities. However, many of those seeking shelter were beginning to spend the whole night in shelters so this argument was no longer valid. The War Cabinet therefore decided to increase the comfort of all shelters, including smaller ones. In conjunction with the Ministry of Home Security, seventy-nine stations were fitted with bunks for night-time shelters. Special sanitary equipment and health clinics were introduced, as well as over a hundred canteens. Eleven tons of food were delivered daily by special trains during the early days of the Blitz to feed the nearly 200,000 people who took shelter in the Underground.

The government also decided to utilise existing structures for shelters, such as strong buildings and railway arches. Some disused tunnels and closed stations were adapted as permanent shelters. They issued police notices to stop the public using other tunnels in London that ran under

52. Not all Underground stations were provided with bunks in the early days of their use as shelters, and some people slept on the tracks.

the Thames. This included the Greenwich, Woolwich, Blackwell and Rotherhithe tunnels. The notices informed the public that the tunnels were not safe during an air raid and that no vehicle or person was allowed into them once an air raid had begun.

Many people had tried taking cover in railway arches but found them not suitable for this purpose. Perhaps the best known of the railway shelters were the Tilbury Arches in Stepney. They were part of a complex of cellars and vaults that were taken over by the council as protection for 3,000 people. They had been used as shelters in the First World War.

As had happened at Liverpool Street, some groups encouraged those sheltering to enter the unofficial part of the complex. The area became one of the largest of London's shelters, housing from 14,000 to 16,000 people at night. In the unofficial parts it was very dirty and was used by large groups of undesirables. Sightseers from the better-off parts of the city would arrive to look at the worst parts of the shelter. The conditions in the Tilbury Arches were a trigger for the agitation for better conditions in shelters.

Improvements to the Stepney shelter led to problems in October, when the public were excluded while work was going on. An air raid warning had been sounded and the shelter had not opened straight away. A party of people tried to rush the ARP control office in Stepney, leading to a fight with the police, who used their batons and made a number of arrests. The *Daily Worker* newspaper complained about the police action but the Home Secretary said that it was justified.

The Underground was never comfortable; many of those sheltering slept on the tracks or the platform. In rare cases, such as in closed stations, bunks were fitted. What the public did feel was a sense of security and of all being in it together. There were inevitable dangers; many of the tunnels ran under the Thames and, as previously mentioned, anti-flood doors were fitted in case a bomb should cause a breach in the tunnels.

The London bombing was causing mayhem to the capital's railway system. Apart from the viaduct at Waterloo, the LNER shed at Marylebone was so badly damaged that its upper floors vanished. Its basement remained full of debris for some time afterwards. St Pancras lost 2½ acres of roof along with two signal boxes. Fenchurch Street station was closed eight times because of the bombing.

53. Floodgates were fitted to a number of Underground stations in case bomb damage caused the influx of water. These gates can still be seen at Baker Street station at the top of the escalators to the Bakerloo Line.

It wasn't only buildings that suffered. When the 8.45 from Liverpool approached the city, the driver was confronted with a huge crater that opened up in front of him. The locomotive and tender fell into the pit, killing the driver and the fireman. The coaches, which were full of soldiers, were flung around the area behind the engine. Luckily, only the guard and one passenger were slightly injured.

The evening of 14 October was to see one of the worst incidents on the London Underground during the war, at Balham – one of the stations being used as a shelter to escape the bombing. The platform was 13 meters below ground so was thought to be safe from the bombs. Just after 8.00 pm, a bomb hit the road above the station, causing a massive crater. It also fractured a water main. The railway tunnel was flooded with water and mud, killing sixty-seven people (various sources cite from sixty-four to sixty-eight deaths) and injuring more than seventy.

54. In October 1940, a bomb exploded in the Balham Underground station, which was being used as a shelter. Nearly seventy people died. The memorial plaque to the dead stands at the top of the escalators to the Northern Line platforms.

There were further problems above ground as a bus fell into the crater, causing more injuries. The crater became larger as the ground gave way beneath it. It took months to clear the site. Bodies were still being found as late as December. The line didn't reopen until mid-January 1941.

London always seems to get the most publicity for the damage from bombing but the LMS records for the London area list the greatest number of incidents for one night at twenty-three. Liverpool had forty-three in one night and Manchester sixty-nine. On the morning of 15 November, the railwaymen in Coventry found twelve places that had been damaged and in need of repair. Much of Coventry station was out of use for two days after that.

The problem was raised at the highest level when it was discussed by the War Cabinet on 13 September. At the meeting, the Prime Minister said, 'As you know, there has been a considerable amount of enemy bombing of railways and termini in the London area. We have been watching the general effects of this bombing to learn lessons from it.' The meeting heard a report from the Railway Executive Committee, who stated that the problems were the congestion of rolling stock in marshalling yards and the delayed action of unexploded bombs. The answer was to empty

55. Driver Blake standing by LMS Ivatt locomotive No. 4423, built at Crewe.

marshalling yards quickly, but this depended on dealing with unexploded bombs promptly. The Minister of Transport stated that there was a serious shortage of skilled gangs who were able to deal with the bombs.

There was also input from the Ministry of Home Security when Major O.G. Villiers reported that so far the enemy had not shown any intention of targeting important junctions further afield, such as at Reading. The attacks on London, however, showed that the enemy had a profound knowledge of the railway system in the capital. The bombing was very accurate, achieving direct hits on stations, junctions and rail lines. This was causing the severance of communication between suburban areas.

There were further problems in transport between the northern and southern railways. The Great Northern section of the LNER normally moved fifty to sixty trains a day to the Southern Railway. On one particular day, only four were able to get through London. There were 5,000 to 6,000 wagons held up on the LNER system waiting to be transferred to the Southern. The LMS had, however, been able to move traffic to the Southern system by using points south-west of London.

The backlog of traffic due to the bombing in London was causing even more concentration of traffic in marshalling yards, which then presented the enemy with further targets for bombing. There were also attacks in Liverpool in September and when a bomb fell near Liverpool Central station, it exploded in a tunnel of the Mersey Railway between two six-coach trains that had been stabled in the sidings. All of the coaches were damaged but only one beyond repair. The line was still able to be used.

Later the same week, another bomb landed on the south side of Park Tunnel, 400 yards from Birkenhead Park station. It collapsed the sides of the tunnel, blocking both lines. A shuttle service of buses replaced trains on the route for eight weeks until the tunnel was repaired.

The marshalling yards were an easy target because of their size. At Clapham Junction, for instance, there were twelve platforms for the twelve lines from London, which meant that it was one of the widest stretches of running lines in the country, covering an area of 35 acres. There were a large number of sidings in Clapham Yard, along with four signal boxes and two sheds that gave covered accommodation for repairs. The sidings were large enough for 640 vehicles, and held much of the steam stock for Waterloo. There were 425 staff, and 120 trains an hour passed through at peak time. The Big Four all had trains passing through. The enemy did not need intelligence information about Clapham Junction; it must have been easily spotted from the air.

The vulnerability of large glass-roofed railway buildings was evident when St Pancras station was bombed. The glass roof measured 2½ acres and most of it was shattered on 16 October 1940. It is hard to imagine what it must have been like to see that amount of broken glass raining down from above.

There was a meeting of the War Cabinet on 21 October to discuss the cost of the railways. The question of raising fares was mentioned as there was a feeling that if the railways were not kept financially sound during the conflict, they would face serious problems once the war ended. It was suggested that workmen's tickets and fares on the London Passenger Transport system should not be raised. Serious concerns were raised about this but it was thought that wages had risen enough to cover the increase. Discussion also took place as to whether there was a case for reducing the preferential margin on government traffic while not interfering with cheap tickets for members of the forces.

An interesting debate during the meeting considered whether industry might pass on the cost of war damage to the consumer. However, a new compensation scheme treated war damage as a capital charge, although it was uncertain how this would apply to the railways. It was agreed to begin negotiations with the railway companies to devise a set of modifications of the scheme.

A further War Cabinet meeting in October again discussed the Tilbury Arches shelter in Stepney. The Secretary of State for Foreign Affairs, Viscount Halifax, had visited the shelter and given a favourable account of the conditions there – most probably after the improvements were carried out.

In November, Mr Herbert Morrison, Minister of Home Security, announced that the deep shelter accommodation in the London Underground was to be extended by further tunnelling. Short tunnels were to be dug leading off the main tunnels. Although this would provide deep shelters for many more people, Mr Morrison realised it was impractical to provide them for the whole of the urban population. It was said that if the London Underground railway system was doubled and

56. A down train at Welshpool. Wales was one of the areas used as a reception point for a number of evacuees.

new tunnels and stations were used for no other purpose than sleeping shelters, it would only be big enough for one in six of the population of London. Wherever it was possible to provide deep shelters, as in more tunnelling in the Underground or in the use of natural sites in other parts of the country, it would be done.

When a landmine fell near London Bridge in December, the station was evacuated. Although the army dealt with bombs, landmines were the responsibility of the navy. The mine was close to a signal box and despite the station being evacuated, the signalman stayed in his box while the mine was defused. It was a clear sign of how the railway staff often put the safety of the railway system above their own.

The problem with the amount of glass in signal boxes was shown in December 1940, when the stationmaster was on duty at Manchester's Victoria West Junction signal box. He was on the telephone at 11.50 pm when there was a blue flash and an explosion. The window facing the station blew in and the glass wrapped around his head, but as it was covered in cellophane, he was saved from serious injury.

* * *

Apart from the attacks on the port and town, Southampton had other problems to cope with by the end of the year. Supplies of perishable food that had been sent to the town were backing up. In many cases, the shops where the food was bound for had been bombed and so could not take delivery of it. Many of the shop owners could not be contacted and the goods were accumulating in railway wagons. Eventually, there was an embargo on any more being sent to the town until the Ministry of Food could dispose of what was already there.

The number of people who had been bombed out in Southampton or who had just left to escape the bombing posed another problem for the railway system. Special trains had to be laid on to take those who had left back to the town each day for work. Then they had to be taken home again in the evening.

The serious bombing in London led to some attempts at restricting the entry of trains into the capital. The LMS began to stop their trains at Watford and then transfer passengers on to electric trains for Euston. The other companies followed suit. The LNER stopped their trains at Finsbury Park but this was so close to King's Cross to be pointless. The SR stopped trains at Woking, but the GWR refused to stop their trains at Ealing Broadway.

In addition to the railways being in continuous danger from bombing during the conflict, they were still prone to the kinds of accidents that had blighted rail travel since its earliest days, despite having reduced speed limits imposed. In 1939, the speeds had been decreased to almost First World War standards. Because there were fewer trains running, they made more stops and starts, and this dragged down the average speeds even more. A train from London to Manchester, for instance, could take an hour longer than its pre-war time as it now had to stop at every station.

Pre-war attempts at streamlining trains to increase speed had led to valances being fitted below the running plate. In some cases, such as with the LNER Pacifics, including the *Golden Eagle* and the *Sea Eagle*, the valances were removed during the war. The loss of speed from removing streamlining was inconsequential in wartime and the removal of the valances also exposed the driving wheel for inspection.

There were other advantages in reducing the speed of trains, the main one being that slower trains did less damage to the tracks. This meant that less maintenance was needed and fewer materials used for repairs. It was also easier to manage trains moving over the same lines if they were all travelling at the same speed. Trains could follow each other on the same lines closer together than those travelling at different speeds.

There is a general belief that during the war, the names of all railway stations were removed. The order of the Minister of Home Security about signs related to those seen from the public highway or from the air. According to a report in *The Times*, 'excessive zeal at many railway stations had removed every name, even those on seats or lamps'. There had also been cases where, by September 1940, names on posters advertising resorts hundreds of miles away from the station had been removed.

There were suggestions as to how to identify where a train was stopping, such as loud speakers or just having a member of staff shouting out the name of the station. Some passengers would note the number of stops before setting off on a journey but signal stops could then make this difficult. There were also cases of passengers getting off the train at a signal stop, thinking they were in a station, and falling on to the line.

By October, there was a level of backtracking by the railway companies. Steps were being taken to restore the station names, but due to the numbers involved, printed paper signs had to be used until more permanent ones could be fitted. These temporary signs still had to comply with Ministry of Transport signage regulations. This solved the problem of station identification during daylight hours but it was still difficult when alighting at stations during the blackout.

On 4 November 1940, at Norton Fitzwarren, near Taunton, the 9.50 express on the GWS from Paddington to Penzance was derailed at 4.00 am. There were twenty-seven fatalities; many had been asleep because of the late hour. The train was crowded with passengers, a number of them servicemen. The engine had come off the line and the first four carriages had telescoped. *The Times* of 5 November listed twenty-four dead, which was the number known at the time. Many of the dead were sailors but a woman and two children were also amongst the fatalities. The driver had survived the accident and had run to the nearby station to put the signal at 'danger' to stop any more trains coming through.

There is no doubt that any crash at that time was instantly blamed on enemy action. However, a GWR official said that the cause of this incident could not be found until the wreckage was cleared but he was certain it was an accident and not due to enemy action or sabotage. A sailor who survived said that he thought it was caused by a bomb. One passenger said that she had seen aircraft wings, but this turned out to be wreckage from the train.

The reason for the accident became clear from the Ministry of War Transport (MoWT) investigation under Lieutenant Colonel A.H.L. Mount. The results were reported in the *Manchester Guardian* on 28 December. It had apparently been due to an unaccountable lapse of concentration by P.W. Stacey, the driver, who had forty years' experience on the GWR. Stacey was looking out for signals on the main line but the train was actually on the relief line. It was thought that this was due to the blackout.

*   *   *

As winter approached, there had been an outcry about shortages of coal for both the railway and the public. The government issued statements regarding the situation and claimed that there was no shortage. There were ample supplies but it was the distribution that was the problem. Numerous trucks full of coal were stuck in sidings waiting to be unloaded. All of it needed to be unloaded by hand, and this was taking time.

Before the war, the railway system had been swamped with thousands of privately owned coal trucks, many poorly maintained. Evidence of this could be seen when looking at a mineral train in a railway yard or when passing on a track. The sturdiest and best maintained trucks would bear the initials of a railway company. The majority would have the names of collieries, coal merchants, industrial coal users or gas and coke companies on them. They were either stood waiting to be returned to their owners or to be unloaded, which all made distribution more difficult.

A scheme was devised to fine private truck owners for not unloading them quickly enough. Eventually, the trucks were pooled, which made things easier. Nevertheless, the problem largely remained of getting them unloaded. The government claimed that in November there were about 3,000 and sometimes up to 4,000 full coal trucks waiting to be unloaded in sidings in the Manchester area alone, a situation that must have been evident in other parts of the country.

The railways had previously kept their own mineral and goods wagons in what was called the Common User Pool. After 1939, there was a requirement to total up the number of wagons passing at exchange stations from one line to another and the handing back of empties. This meant that each company had the same number of wagons that it had originally possessed. It was numbers that mattered, not whose trucks they were.

580,000 RAILWAYMEN
are maintaining
a Vital National Service

To the task of maintaining this service, the British Railways have brought the skilled assistance of more than half a million railwaymen and women, all animated by the spirit of service and the will to win ; they have also brought the mighty contribution of

50,000 Miles of Track	20,000 Locomotives
60,000 Passenger Vehicles	1,250,000 Freight Vehicles
76 Docks, Harbours and Wharves	11,000 Horses
25,000 Horse-Drawn Vehicles	10,000 Road Vehicles

Primarily this vast machine is harnessed to the tremendous requirements of the Forces and of Home Defence ; at the same time the British Railways continue to provide the public with the best services possible.

Issued by
THE RAILWAY EXECUTIVE COMMITTEE

57. A Railway Executive Committee advertisement explaining the vital work done by the railways during the war.

There was another problem with the movement of coal in that the layout of colliery sidings had mainly been designed for four-wheel goods trucks and comparatively short trains. It would have been much quicker and more convenient to be able to use high capacity wagons and longer trains that could be run at higher speeds. This would require goods vehicles with continuous brakes and more powerful locomotives.

Although this could be developed quite easily during peacetime, it would have been much more difficult during the war. After the war, however, there wouldn't be the need to switch to this more dependable system as there wasn't such a pressing demand for coal.

In contrast to the cutbacks in the production of railway trucks and locomotives in the early years of the war, there was a steady flow of new rolling stock for the deep level London Underground. There were ninety-nine non-driving motor coaches and 271 trailers built by the Birmingham Railway Carriage and Wagon Company Limited. There were also 644 driving motor coaches and 107 non-driving motor coaches built by the Metropolitan-Cammell Carriage and Wagon Company Limited. All the motor coaches were of the same horsepower and generally the rush hour trains consisted of seven cars semi-permanently coupled together, which included a four-car unit comprising two driving motor coaches, a non-driving coach and a trailer, and a three-car unit with two driving motor coaches and a trailer. Then for non-rush hour traffic, it was possible to run either a three- or a four-car train by splitting the seven-car unit.

As well as the deep level stock, there were also 573 vehicles, of which 189 were motor coaches and 270 trailers from the Gloucester Railway Carriage and Wagon Company, and ninety-eight motor coaches and sixteen trailers from the Birmingham Company. These were for the District and Metropolitan lines. There had been twenty trains built for the Metropolitan Line by the Vickers Company, who were better known for making guns and ammunition. The trains were electric and had been built just after the First World War. The Metropolitan Line terminated at Baker Street and the trains were named after local celebrities connected with the area.

One of these was No. 8, *Sherlock Holmes*, and No. 5 was named after John Hampden, a supporter of the Parliamentary side in the Civil War.

58. One of the twenty old Vickers engines that ran on the Metropolitan Railway that were named after local celebrities. This is No. 12, *Sarah Siddons*, shown at Uxbridge. Siddons was a famous eighteenth-century actress. (*Neil Pruitt*)

The *John Hampden* is now in the London Transport Museum. For many years, a Vickers shell stood by the First World War memorial in the station. Baker Street station was also the site of the London Transport rifle range. During the war it was used to train members of the Special Operation Executive, whose headquarters was at No. 64 Baker Street.

The preparations for retaking Europe began early in the war and the army had set up training areas at locations that indicated the important role that the railways would play if invasion came. One was at Longmoor, near Aldershot, which had been used by railway troops since before the First World War and was converted into a training ground for the railway units of the Territorial Army. Another was at Melbourne, Derbyshire, which had once been a branch line on the LMS.

There were a number of locomotives at Longmoor for the men to train on. These were mainly old LNER engines that had arrived during the

59. Another view of the *Sarah Siddons*, which is now used for heritage events. Another of the engines, No. 5, *John Hampden*, can be seen in the London Transport Museum at Covent Garden. (*Georgie Duane*)

war. There were also a number of old GWR mainline coaches, four ex-Caledonian Railway non-corridor coaches and some ex-LMS coaches, as well as an assortment of wagons that were used for carrying tanks. Most of the vehicles were painted dark green.

The railway units also needed practice in loading and unloading ships, which was not possible at their training bases, so a new training area was set up on the coast for this purpose. This was at Faslane, near Glasgow. A branch line was put in to serve the base that was connected to the LNER main lines but was controlled by the army. The Royal Engineers who ran the site were mainly ex-railwaymen, not always from the British railways.

Chapter 5

1941

There were more Austerity locomotives built in 1941. The LMS type 2-8-0, which had been adopted by the Ministry of Supply as an Austerity engine, had been in production since 1940, but Nos. 500 to 623 were built from 1941 to 1942 by the North British Locomotive Company.

A number of the Austerity engines commissioned by the War Department were based on engines from one of the railway companies. The ROD type 2-8-0 was modelled on a design by Mr J.G. Robinson for the Great Central Railway. The design had also been used in the First World War. There were ninety-two of these engines supplied to the LNER but they were requisitioned and sent overseas. Some of these were later returned and sold to the LNER and the GWR.

The Sudan type 4-6-2 locomotive was ordered from the North British Locomotive Company by the Sudan government. There were fifty-five made, which were then taken over by the War Department and used on

60. One of the many Austerity locomotives built during the war. This is No. 8042, built for the LMS.

the East African coast line. The North British Locomotive Company must have been very busy in 1941 as they also built six 4-6-4 tank locomotives for the Malay States Railways. Malaya was then taken over by the Japanese, so the engines were sent to Palestine instead.

The 0-4-0 diesel locomotive was ordered by the Ministry of Supply in 1941. Ten were built by Andrew Barclay Sons & Co, Kilmarnock, and ten by the Drewry Car Company, Preston. Some of these went ashore in Normandy on landing crafts and were pulled across the sand on tank conveyers. These were the only ones that were ordered, built from 1941 to 1945.

In January 1941, the *Manchester Guardian* published a report on the use of the Underground as a shelter. The article didn't name the station involved but no doubt it was representative of the Underground as a whole. The stations could accommodate a large number of people but in most cases, according to the article, they had not achieved warmth, ventilation, bunks, canteens or medical facilities. This was not the case in every station. Those with bunks had three-tiered beds with a sacking or metal base. The occupants' own bedclothes could be left on the bunk to save carrying them back and forth. The upper bunks had lights for readers and the lower bunks could accommodate three people sitting side by side, allowing for conversation.

It wasn't only Londoners who were sheltering in the station, said the newspaper; there were refugees from Gibraltar, a Norwegian, a French Jewess, a Polish woman and two German Jewish refugees, one of whom was a picture dealer who gave his address as the Tube station and had letters delivered there.

The shelters were cared for by shelter marshals, who were either women or elderly men from various walks of life, the men mainly retired. They would often collect donations for help towards canteen facilities or celebrations at Christmas time. The marshals knew all the occupants. There was a doctor who did his rounds and a Red Cross bay, where the sick could be isolated. The report also mentioned the friendliness amongst the shelterers despite the trying conditions.

Although all four of the rail companies had London termini, it was the Southern Railway that was the most damaged by bombing. To keep the services running as smoothly as possible, control centres were set up at central points, which were manned twenty-four hours a day. The centres were based in various departments of the railway. There was a separate section dealing with air raid damage. All the sections were in touch by telephone. If the information was that a bomb had dropped, steps were taken to find out the level of damage. If the person reporting the bomb thought that serious damage had occurred, the trains would be stopped and engineers sent to examine it. Details would then be passed on to another section, which would be in control of running alternative services.

There were a number of lines that had hardly been used or were uneconomic before the war and these could offer alternative routes when the well-used mainlines were put out of action by bombing. There were already alternative services taking place on some of the railway sections where passenger trains were being cancelled to allow more coal trains to run. On the LMS, the only cuts definitely decided had been in the Birmingham area, where about a dozen local trains were cancelled. None of the trains running into London were affected.

On the Southern, there was a reduction of passenger services on the Crystal Palace to Blackfriars route and some changes in train times. The LNER cut trains between the old Great Northern suburban stations and Moorgate, where passenger trains were suspended indefinitely. Moorgate had closed in October 1940 due to bomb damage and didn't reopen until after the war. There were no cuts on the GWR.

Development on the railways did not stop completely during the war. In January 1941, a new station was opened on the London Underground at Highgate. It was closely connected with the overground railway, lying underneath the surface station of the LNER. The two stations were connected by escalator and the Underground station was on the Northern Line.

The station had been complete in September the previous year apart from the escalators. The platforms were then used as shelters from the bombing. The station was accessed by special trains from other stations. This began as a semi-official shelter and facilities were provided on a voluntary basis by London Transport staff. Once the station became an official shelter it was supplied with a canteen. There were four entrances: two in Archway Road, one in Priory Gardens and one in Wood Lane.

61. Moorgate in London was one of the stations that closed early in the war, in 1940, and remained closed until 1946.

Although the station was opened during the war, a further planned set of escalators from Archway Road was postponed until after the war ended.

The surface station was used by steam trains running to the city via Finsbury Park. The overground service between East Finchley and Highgate was stopped a few months after the Underground station opened. This was an example of how duplication of services was ended as passengers on the LNER services from Alexandra Palace and Muswell Hill were able to reach the city by changing to the Underground at Highgate.

Although the use of dining cars on trains had been discontinued during the war, in January, Ernest Lemon developed the provision of canteens for troops on trains because of the difficulty of them obtaining food when in transit. The canteens were fitted into the end compartments of two carriages and could be quickly assembled or removed again within twelve minutes. They were staffed by the YMCA and the Salvation Army. The idea was put forward by the Army Welfare and Education Department, who were also looking into the possibility of providing hostels close to railway stations for soldiers who needed to rest while waiting for trains. There were already some of these but it was hoped to expand the scheme.

The London Underground may have had a higher level of protection than the overground system, but it was not always safe. When a bomb fell on Waterloo on 5 January, it destroyed the lifts to the Underground and blocked the entrance. Arch 258, beneath Waterloo station, was also used as an air raid shelter and was even the venue for a wartime concert performed by musicians from Morley College. There was almost an underground city at Waterloo, with large catacombs opening into each other. These were ruled by Mr Greenfield, the station manager, who was also the chief warden. The area sheltered more than 6,000 people, with 500 of them actually living there. These were families who had been bombed out of their homes and had nowhere else to go. The residents had bunks and some even brought items of furniture. Part of the shelter was also turned into offices for the headquarters staff from Deepdene just in case there was an invasion and they had to move back to London.

62. The railway convalescent home at Dawlish, 1945. No doubt many of the patrons at this time were there due to war injuries.

In February, there was an attack on a GWR train at Swansea. The fireman of the Landore to Swansea train was lying underneath while coupling it. When the bombs began to fall, he stayed underneath the tender for protection. While he was there, the glass canopy over the platform crashed to the ground. He stayed under the train for an hour. During the attack, the signals were all at danger, so the train couldn't leave the station. However, there had been a circular in October 1939 stating that if it was safe to do so, a signalman or the stationmaster could allow the train to leave the station during an attack. The train left, keeping its speed down to 15 miles an hour.

In February 1941, there was a major step forward for women employed on the railways when twelve female porters began work at Preston station. They wore blue armbands with a white LMS logo, which was the only uniform they had at the time. Although this was an important development, it was not entirely unusual as there had been women porters at the station in the First World War.

A number of railway workers did fire-watching duty after work. A press report from this time told of a shunter and a young boy who fought fires continuously for twelve hours at the railway of an unnamed West Country town. The pair extinguished a string of incendiary bombs that had fallen amongst railway wagons. They saved a load of timber from a burning lorry while the raid went around them. They then helped deal with injured men from a gas works and with putting out fires in houses and a hotel.

There were numerous stories of the bravery of rail workers during the raids. Another pair,

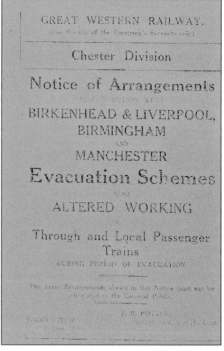

63. A notice of changes to rail services in the north of England during evacuation. (*Gillian Mawson*)

who were messengers, saved a plan room and a boiler house when they organised a chain of men with buckets to bring water from three stirrup pumps. A railway fitter removed seventeen loaded vehicles and six loaded trailers from a burning warehouse while it was being bombed. There must have been numerous similar examples of bravery that were never reported.

The number of evacuees continued to rise into 1941 with the ever-present threat of invasion after the Battle of Britain, and 746,000 evacuees were moved from the east and south coasts by 988 special trains in four days.

The moving of much of the coastal traffic to the west may have saved ships from attacks in the North Sea and the English Channel, but the docks in the west were not immune from attack. Swansea suffered severely. In February, heavy raids blocked High Street station in the city centre but the damage to the docks was much less serious. Cardiff, Newport and Barry also suffered some level of damage.

There was a higher concentration of raids on the Mersey River but they were never successful enough to seriously damage the docks. Repairs were quickly carried out and the docks were defended well. The rail services to the Liverpool docks were controlled by the LMS offices in Crewe and Manchester, although the Manchester office had been as good as destroyed the previous year.

The same could not be said for the Mersey Railway when heavy damage was caused by landmines at Birkenhead Park station and nearby Green Lane station in March. There was also damage to Birkenhead Central workshops. The booking hall and offices at Birkenhead Park station were completely wrecked along with the platform buildings. One span of Duke Street rail bridge at Birkenhead docks was destroyed along with a six-coach train in the carriage shed. A large crater was made in the middle of the tracks at the Hamilton Square end of Birkenhead Central station. The service from Liverpool via Park to West Kirby recommenced five days later, and to New Brighton a day after that.

There were already a number of women working on the railways by this time but in March, Ernest Bevin, Minister of Labour and National Service, called for 100,000 women to enrol for war work. They were needed to replace men who had gone into the forces. To encourage those who had children, he announced the expansion of nurseries. Bevin thought that every two men who had left would need to be replaced by three women.

There was an obvious need for women on the railways and there was an incentive for women from railway families to follow their fathers or husbands into the industry. Indeed, women often found it easier to get jobs on the railway if they had family already working there. There had always been a view that working on the railways was a good job and it was often thought of as a job for life.

There was a very strict process for progressing through the ranks. One of the jobs that appeared to be suitable for women was the role of engine cleaner. This was a problem, though, because it was traditionally regarded as a job for young men as the first step on the ladder to becoming an engine driver. The normally slow process of promotion had to change as some women progressed swiftly on to jobs that had previously taken men some time to achieve, although the men who remained working the wartime railways were also likely to be promoted more quickly.

Many railwaymen were being called up at this time as their jobs were no longer seen as reserved. This often led to those who remained being moved up to the next grade, leaving their previous jobs to be taken by women. When there was a shortage of guardsmen, for instance, men would be promoted from jobs such as ticket collecting, and those roles would then be filled by women.

The LMS also began to recruit women to their police force. There were even some female detectives. They would travel on trains as passengers while looking out for any wrongdoings that were going on, including being on the lookout for pilfering staff.

One of the places that Bevin's ladies were employed was Leeds. The city's worst raids of the war took place in March 1941, although for such an important industrial area, it got off relatively lightly. Leeds had very strong railway connections, having had at one time the largest concentration of railway engine builders in the country. The city's industries had struggled during the 1930s, but the war led to an upturn for many, with the government orders for locomotives.

One of these companies was Kitson's, whose production of engines had declined in the pre-war days when they faced financial hardship.

64. Women took over a number of jobs on the railways during the war, including signal duties.

Their wartime orders kept them going. Other companies in the city turned to wartime production, with Burton's tailors producing uniforms, and Oxley's mineral water company turning its hand to Coca-Cola for American troops based in the area.

Apart from railway vehicles, the biggest wartime production work was in munitions. The Olympia factory made Blackburn aircraft, and Avro aircraft were also produced in the city. Vickers Armstrong manufactured guns and tanks at their factory in Crossgates, but didn't have enough capacity there. To supplement the output, the Royal Ordnance Factory had been built in 1939-40 on the 60-acre Barnbow site, with a large input from the railway. The site had been an armament factory up until 1932 and many of the women who had worked there in the First World War now returned.

* * *

In March, there was a heavy raid on Waterloo, resulting in all rail traffic having to stop at Clapham Junction. All the lines at Waterloo were out of service at 9.00 pm on Saturday. There were large bomb craters in the arches alongside the lines. All the steam lines were working again by 9.37 am the next day, and the electric lines were working by 4.00 pm on Monday. The story was the same everywhere, with bomb damage often repaired either the same day or by the next day.

In April, Charing Cross Station and hotel was bombed. A porter named Gillet told Mr Basset, the stationmaster, that he had tripped over a landmine. The mine was hanging by its parachute from Hungerford Bridge, close to a signal box that was still occupied by the signalman. There were no telephones working so the porter ran through the streets during the raid to fetch the fire brigade. There was a serious fire on platform four of the station. Although all the station staff were evacuated, the signalman, Mr Briggs, who was 67, stayed in the box next to the mine. The fire had meanwhile spread to the hotel and was being fought by the staff, a railway guard, two Canadian soldiers and an airman, demonstrating that any member of the forces would rush to help in an emergency. While all this was going on, a naval officer dealt with the mine.

There were a number of air raids on Northern Ireland in April and May 1941, and a large number of British troops were based there, later followed by a number of US troops who were arriving on a regular basis. This was because of the danger of a German invasion of Ireland. There were also a number of camps for evacuees from Gibraltar. These factors all added to the workload of the railways in having to move large groups of people.

The railways in Northern Ireland had a connection with the mainland in that the LMS had some control of them there after they had taken over the Belfast and Northern Counties Railway (BNCR). There was also a military railway training depot, with its headquarters at Whitehead, County Antrim. Detachments from there had been sent out to other areas.

There was a mobile railway workshop at Whitehead, which was based on a train and consisted of Southern Railway coaches from Ashford. The workshop was responsible for armour plating petrol-driven trolleys. They were used to control anti-social behaviour of dissident groups as there was still a religious divide in Northern Ireland. They were also used to carry army stores.

65. A Great Northern Railway (Ireland) locomotive at Belfast shed. The LMS were the only one of the Big Four to have lines in Ireland.

By this stage of the war, the Luftwaffe were concentrating their attacks on the ports of Britain, and in April they revisited Coventry, which had been badly damaged by bombing raids the previous year. They were also specifically targeting towns and cities where there was armament production.

66. A Dundalk engine on the Great Northern Railway in Northern Ireland.

A scheme had been introduced shortly after the beginning of the war whereby certain types of rail vans were pooled, but now, due to increasing demands on these resources, it was felt that additional co-ordination was needed to deal with the movement of other types of rolling stock and equipment. An inter-company organisation was to oversee the movement of wagons, vans, sheets and ropes.

In 1941, the GWR was employing greater numbers of women, seeing a rise from 2,000 to 8,000 by 1942. This may have been due, in part, to the retirement of Mr C.B. Collett. Many women were sent from the Labour Exchange. Also, women and girls who were single were being sent from other parts of the country, such as the East End of London, under the National Service scheme. Many of them ended up at Swindon, having no idea what job they would do once they arrived. They would be found digs to stay in or they lived in workers' camps.

All of the Big Four railway companies were now employing more women, with some being given high power jobs. Three women employed at the Euston Enquiry Bureau – Dorothy Segesser, Marjorie Berrill and Doris Hillier – had to pass an exhaustive test to prove their knowledge of the train service and skills in using a microphone. They were about to become train announcers for the LMS.

Delays on the railways caused by the bomb attacks were now becoming regular occurrences, but alternative methods of transport were also experiencing serious problems. On one particular day, the road between Clapham Junction and Waterloo had a traffic queue a mile long as the road was blocked with fire hoses. The journey between the two stations on a bus took three and a half hours.

On 23 April, all communication between Plymouth and Devonport was cut off. An emergency service was set up, which was arranged through the Great Western District, but it meant that the trains were running on Southern tracks.

A study in the *Railway Magazine* showed that since the introduction of a new timetable in May, the number of buffet cars on trains had been steadily increasing. Buffett cars had been withdrawn in the first few months of the war but reintroduced in late 1939 and early 1940. On their reintroduction, there were 365 trains equipped to offer meals and light refreshments daily. By May 1941, this had increased to 440 daily. The

67. Repair work taking place on the GWR at Lampton, Hounslow.

LNER was the leading service in this, rising from forty-two to ninety a day. Not all the buffet cars were for the use of the public, however. On the express service between King's Cross and Edinburgh, the buffet was only for service personnel. The same service was used on the Euston to Glasgow express.

One of the shortest journey times on a train provided with a buffet car was the LNER service between Newcastle and Sunderland. The journey took only twenty-one minutes. This was thought to be a record until it was discovered that a Southern Railway service between Victoria and East Croydon, which took ten and a half minutes, also had a buffet car.

The amount of damage inflicted on the Southern Railway was evident by the spring. From September the previous year up until May 1941, there had been ninety-two incidents, and this was just in the 2½ miles between Waterloo and Queen's Road stations.

Heavy raids on Liverpool in May again had an effect on the Mersey Railway. James Street station buildings at street level were practically destroyed and the lifts put out of action. The station was closed to trains for six days and the main entrance and lifts were not opened again for months. Half the company's rolling stock had been destroyed in a six-month period but the train system was maintained at almost full strength and the cross-river traffic between Liverpool and Birkenhead never stopped running.

In June, a 2,000lb bomb fell on the railway booking office in Southampton. It went through the roof and the floor, but the only casualty was a dog. Because of the extent of the damage and the fire that had started, it was thought that the bomb had exploded. The staff were sent back to work unaware that the bomb was still intact under the floor. The landlord of the nearby Mason's Arms came over and told them that he hadn't heard the bomb explode, resulting in the staff being evacuated again before the bomb was found.

An exhibition of railway photographs organised by the Big Four companies and London Transport was displayed at Charing Cross Underground station. The exhibition aroused so much public interest that it was decided it should go on tour, for which a luggage van was transformed into a well-lit picture gallery. The exhibition was to visit twenty-eight stations and spend three days at each, showing images of the evacuation of schoolchildren, the evacuation of Dunkirk and the railway companies' challenges with bad weather and bomb damage. A souvenir booklet was issued of the display at a cost of sixpence.

Of the Big Four, the Great Western Railway suffered some of the most serious accidents during the wartime period. After the accident in November the previous year at Norton Fitzwarren, the next occurred at Dolphin Junction near Slough on 2 July. Five people died when a passenger train from Plymouth had a head-on collision with a goods train. It happened at 3.00 am. The train, being from Plymouth, had a number of naval personnel on board and three of the five fatalities were sailors. *The Times* mentioned that many of the passengers on board the Plymouth train were servicemen on their way to London on leave. The accident happened on the crossover point from the main to the slow line. Rescue work was mainly carried out by servicemen, some of whom had been passengers. They were aided by the ARP and other civil defence men from Slough and the Home Guard.

At this time, the press were less inclined to publish rumours as to what had caused the accident as they had been in the past. The possibility of any damage being caused by enemy action was not given in press reports as it could inform the enemy; they had to be certain that any disaster was not enemy related before any details were published. The GWR did eventually accept responsibility, but it wasn't until 5 November that a further report appeared in *The Times*. This stated that it had been the signalman, Mr Welch, who was to blame. He said that he had made a mistake by assuming that the goods train had stopped. The investigation, under Major G. Wilson, said there was no reason why the signalman could not have diverted the goods train on to the up line so that the express could pass.

There was a new type of ticket made available in July, when applications were invited for vouchers for special tickets at reduced fares. The scheme was announced by the Ministry of War Transport. The tickets were to be issued to those who wished to travel to spend their summer holidays with

68. The railway war memorial in the bus station outside Euston station. It commemorates those who worked for the London and North Eastern Railway who died in the First World War and those of the London Midland and Scottish in the Second World War. (*Kyra Foley*)

members of their family who had been evacuated. The railway companies had agreed that until the end of September, one ticket valid for eight days would be issued to anyone eligible for a voucher. Applicants had to supply written evidence that they had secured accommodation for the week at their destination, and their application had to be made nine days before the leaving date.

There was a meeting of the War Cabinet in July and one of the items under discussion was the control of the railways. The Minster of War Transport said that the appointment of the Railway Executive Committee as the minister's agents was to ensure the centralised direction of operations under war conditions. The minister then directed his instructions to the management through the committee but the initiative of the company's management was preserved in the day-to-day running of the railways. In certain respects, where closer co-operation between systems such as Central Wagon Control, Central Stores and Purchasing was needed, this had to be imposed on the companies. The minister went on to say that a division of functions between the members of the committee would hopefully bring about improvements.

A well-known name in locomotive design was to retire in July. Mr C.B. Collett, the Chief Mechanical Engineer of the GWR, was to leave Swindon. During his career, he had carried on the good work of his predecessor at Swindon, Mr G.J. Churchward, who had laid the foundation for the design of steam locomotives – the prime favourite for motive power over electric and diesel.

Mr Collett was instrumental in the design of the King class, which met the growing demand for locos due to the increased traffic. He had also built over 250 Hall Grange and Manor 4-6-0 locomotives, using Churchward's Saint class as a basis. For the heaviest freight traffic, he was responsible for the production of the 2-8-2 tanks. Collett was succeeded by Mr F.W. Hawksworth.

The government's pleas for the public to holiday at home seemed to fall on deaf ears as people took every opportunity to get away. The August Bank Holiday attracted thousands of visitors to the seaside and countryside. London stations were as crowded as on any peacetime Bank Holiday weekend. There was also travel in the opposite direction as many people visited London, leading to large crowds on the Thames

Embankment. A railway official explained that, as common carriers, the railways were duty bound to provide facilities for every member of the public issued with a ticket and therefore extra passenger trains had to be run.

The situation was similar in other parts of the country. Despite holiday times being staggered, there were still large crowds of people in places such as Manchester, Birmingham, Liverpool and other cities trying to get away at weekends. Traditional holiday destinations such as Blackpool, Bournemouth and Torquay reported that it was difficult to find accommodation for the numbers of people arriving. Many of the

69. A crowded station in London during the war. Despite government attempts to stop the public travelling at holiday times, the railways were often overrun.

passengers alighting at Brighton were turned away at the station because the area was restricted.

A Ministry of War Transport official said that if pleasure seekers ignored advice, making it necessary to run extra trains, then they may have to wait a considerable time, especially on the return journey. This was because there was no obligation on the part of the railways about the time that passengers were carried.

There was a change to the Railway Executive Committee in August when the chairman, Sir Ralph Wedgwood, resigned. His place was taken by Sir Alan Anderson, who would also hold the new post of Controller of Railways in the Ministry of War Transport. Sir Alan expressed his wish to serve without a salary.

There were constant attacks and damage to the country's railways from the air but in August, Blackpool suffered a very unusual type of damage to its Central station. A large number of military men were based at Blackpool and there was also an RAF training base in the town. On one August day, four 256 Squadron Defiant aircraft took off from the base to practise formation flying. One then returned to base, leaving three flying above the town. The town was packed with holidaymakers, many of whom were close to the railway station, which was near the beach. Consequently, many witnessed the three Defiants veer towards a Botha aircraft. As the Botha approached them the first two Defiants pulled away but the third one collided with it. The Botha crashed on to the Central station, its fuel immediately setting fire to the building. The Defiant landed on a nearby house.

Large crowds filled the roads around the station, hampering the rescue work. Five soldiers were later given awards for bravery for their efforts to help. Central station closed in the 1960s, but inside Blackpool's North Station is a memorial to the railwaymen and women who died in the war and another memorial to a hero from the day the plane crashed, Thomas Beeston, an LMS police officer who saved the life of a young girl. He was awarded a merit badge and ten guineas. The crews of both aircraft were killed, along with eleven civilians.

In addition to the Underground being utilised for wartime shelter, railway tunnels were also used to protect both people and trains from attacks. In October, Kemp Town tunnel at Brighton was used in a trial to

In memory of those who died at

Blackpool Central Station

on August 27th 1941

and the brave efforts of

PC Thomas Beeston (LMS Railway Police),

Public Citizens and Rescue Services

who did all they could to save lives

70. The memorial in Blackpool North Station to those who died at Blackpool Central station when an aircraft crashed on it after colliding with another aircraft.

stable electric trains at night, and in the mornings they were pulled out by steam engines.

The lack of construction of new rolling stock was hampering the LMS in October. Despite not being able to make new locomotives, the company was still expected to supply them to the military. There had been some respite early in the war after France had fallen so quickly that the engines that had been due to be sent there didn't go. By this time, locomotives and diesel shunting engines were needed for Russia, which added to the problem of supply.

There had been an order placed by the LMS for the construction of 100 new 350hp locomotives in December 1940 but by April 1941, manufacture hadn't even been started. The order was later suspended. Since the government had taken over the railways there was some belief that any initiatives put forward by the rail companies were being stifled by civil servants.

The Ministry of Supply had placed an order with the Carriage and Wagon Builders Association for 10,000 freight wagons of 20 ton capacity and 240 2-8-0 locomotives for use by the British Expeditionary Force in France. The wagons were of the four-wheeled covered type, with a weight of 12 tons. They could accommodate forty men or eight horses. They were made of wood, with sliding doors each side, and were to be assembled overseas. They were to supplement the French stock but because of the short time that the British Army spent in France, most of them were never sent.

There was a change in emphasis on the trains in London from October, when it was decided that all trains beginning and ending their journey within the London Passenger Transport area would be third class only, affecting about 5,000 trains. This also extended partly outside London, to Witham in the east, Bishop's Stortford in the north, Guildford in the south and Reading in the west. This was to meet the wartime difficulties of workers travelling into and out of London. The concentration of travellers in London was greater than in any other city and the average journey to and from home was longer. Most of the trains in London had been third class for some time. What remained of separate barriers designating first class compartments were obliterated and the floor rugs that had been in first class were removed.

The year 1941 saw a big change in the railway system. It was the year in which women began to take on more varied and important roles and the number of women employed on the railways increased. There had been a meeting of railway women of the Soviet Union, and in October, they sent greetings 'to the wives, mothers, sisters and daughters of the railwaymen of Great Britain as friends in the common struggle against the hated enemy of all freedom-loving peoples'. A list of ten signatories was headed by Capitolina Chechetkiona, assistant manager of the electric locomotives shed of the Yaroslavsky Railway. The women in Russia

71. The military didn't always get to travel in comfort on the railways during the war, as this image shows.

obviously achieved higher status on the railway earlier than those in Britain. The list included a female stationmaster, an engine driver and an engineer.

Because of the war, there was a change to railway practice that ended a tradition that had been in place for a hundred years. Due to paper salvage, railway tickets were to be proportioned more in line with those of other types of transport or entertainment venues. Tickets had been 1/32 of an inch thick since 1838, but would now be thinner.

Ernest Lemon at the LMS could see the way the railways were going during the conflict. He believed that there was now a lesser need for express trains. The soldiers travelling around the country wanted a cheap, basic level of rail service. Lemon also had serious doubts about the future of the railways after the war. He realised that the restrictions on petrol during the conflict seriously curtailed road travel and the railways were vital. After the war ended, however, there would be more petrol available and road transport would become a serious competitor for the railways. Lemon realised that the railways had only just escaped nationalisation after the First World War and this was still Labour Party policy.

The blackout was strictly enforced on the railway during the conflict but in times of emergency it was soon forgotten. When two trains collided on 30 December 1941 near Eccles station, it was said to be due to poor visibility and weather as well as the blackout. These trains were carrying workers rather than servicemen. Local civil defence workers lit bonfires and used torches to improve visibility while trying to rescue survivors. There were twenty-three fatalities.

On numerous occasions, railway employees went well beyond their normal call of duty without regard for their own safety. One example of this occurred in December and involved a munitions train stabled in a siding near Liverpool. The train received a direct hit from a high explosive bomb. For a number of hours, ten railway employees, led by goods guard George Roberts, worked through the air raid to minimise the danger. Roberts, with another guard, Peter Kilshaw, and a shunter named Evans, uncoupled wagons to remove them from those that were on fire.

While this was going on, driver Robert Bate and his fireman, George Wilkinson, with guard James Rowland, managed to remove wagons in other nearby sidings away from the scene. Another driver, Alexander Ritchie, and fireman William Fowler, took a light engine to pull away wagons on to other tracks away from the fire. No one would have blamed the men for fleeing from the area but it didn't enter their heads to do anything other than try to tackle the situation.

72. Railway stations had a much larger and more varied staff during the war years than they do today, as this image of the staff at Faversham station shows.

Chapter 6

1942

Although Austerity engines had been in production for some years, 1942 was to see a change. The 2-8-2 Austerity locomotive was different from the other Austerity engines in that it was built in America. Locomotives of this type were ordered by the Ministry of Supply and were made by three American companies in 1942. The companies were Baldwin Locomotive Works (BLW), Lima Locomotive Works and the American Locomotive Company (ALCO). The engines

73. The war memorial on platform one at Paddington station. The memorial contains a casket made at Swindon with a list written on velum of those railway employees who died in both world wars. (*Kyra Foley*)

were shipped straight to Suez and then to the Syrian and Palestinian railways.

The Beyer Garratt 4-8-2 and 2-8-4 were built by Beyer, Peacock and Company of Manchester for service in Africa. They were either 3-foot 6-inch, or a metre, gauge. They were used in Kenya, Uganda, Rhodesia, the Gold Coast and the Belgian Congo.

The beginning of the year saw some relaxation in the blackout at stations. Since the Germans had invaded Russia, the number of air attacks had declined. Some station name signs were also replaced. The bombing was not over, however, as was to be seen in the following months.

The might of the Luftwaffe may not have been able to stop the railways running but the British weather could. January saw a severe snowstorm that caused widespread disruption on the LMS and the LNER railways. Heavy snow almost completely stopped the LNER system running. Points were blocked and there were a number of minor derailments. Ten engines were derailed in the Doncaster area alone.

The worst snowfalls were in Scotland, where a number of lines were blocked. The Aberdonioan express from King's Cross had to be diverted via Perth and was hours late. In Aberdeen, two goods trains were buried in snow and were dug out by soldiers. A passenger train from Aberdeen ran into a drift south of Fraserburgh and passengers were trapped for hours. A 9.30 pm train from Glasgow to Euston arrived seventeen hours late. A train carrying 800 war workers, mainly women, from Stoke to Crewe was stranded in a snowdrift for four and a half hours.

In North Yorkshire, a train from Whitby to Scarborough ran into a drift between Ravenscar and Staintondale. Passengers were taken off to the local stationmaster's house and a hotel while LNER engineers and soldiers dug the train out. On the LMS system, the snow was at its worst in Stoke-on-Trent, Crewe, Chester and Liverpool.

The snow was mainly only about a foot deep but it was the kind of snow that was the problem. It was fine powdery snow that drifted on to points and froze them. When soldiers arrived to free the points around Crewe, they found that in the vicinity of the station alone they numbered 235, so it was an arduous task. The situation was the same in other areas and many had to be cleared more than once.

A report by the Select Committee on National Expenditure discussed the loss of output in the country's factories. They found that the main cause was due to the difficulties of worker transport: people often lived 30 miles from their place of employment and had to suffer crowded, tardy and inadequate train services. This often led to them being away from home for up to fifteen hours a day, usually with a long wait for transport after a tiring day's work. The majority of workers suffering such conditions were women and older men.

Another reason for loss of output connected with transport was a delay in the delivery of materials. The report found that not all transport delays were due to the war although many were affected by air raids and troop movements. There was also a legacy of uneconomic working of the railways from the pre-war period. In 1938, the average wagonload carried had been 2.81 tons whilst wagon capacity was 11.25 tons.

The report went on to say that a simple reorganisation of railway running would increase efficiency and free up more manpower, coal and rolling stock. Fully laden wagons and trains would mean less shunting, and marshalling would be avoided. The report claimed that railway transport often led to goods travelling further than they would if they were being taken by road. This was also due to the insistence of the railway companies on maintaining their independence and worrying about what was going to happen after the war.

It was also claimed that the lull in bombing over the previous six months had led to a lax attitude towards encouraging workers to maximise production for the war effort. There had been a loss of momentum in workers' attitudes to doing their bit for the war effort, which had been at its strongest after Dunkirk and during the heavy bombing raids on Britain. It was this feeling that led to a lack of willingness amongst women to leave their homes and work long distances away. Some of those women who were willing to work were hampered by a lack of nursery provision for young children. By the end of 1941, there was childcare capacity for 15,000 children, although in Birmingham alone, there were 70,000 children under 5 years of age.

It was strange, however, that as the report was explaining these details, *The Times* was at the same time reporting how 1941 had been an exceptionally busy year. There had been an urgent call to aid Russia, which was answered by the manufacture of 1,000 steel railway wagons for the country as well as the dispatch of 143 heavy freight locomotives.

There was an unusual item in the press in January when thirteen guardsmen were alleged to have been involved in a scheme to defraud the railways. When soldiers went on leave the railway companies issued them with a leave ticket with the destination written on it. It was discovered that a certain fluid could remove the ink that had been used to write the destination, allowing for a new destination to be added in green ink. The altered tickets were then sold to soldiers going on leave but with destinations much further away than had been originally written on them. The man said to be behind the scheme was Joseph McCudden, who was sentenced to nine months in prison. Edward Francis Waters and Alan Parker each got a six-month sentence. The other guardsmen involved were bound over for two years.

Accidents were still occurring on the railways, which was no surprise considering the increase in the amount of traffic. There was a serious accident in Scotland on 30 January in which thirteen people died when the express from Edinburgh to Glasgow hit light engines at Cowlairs, near Glasgow. The train had been slowing as it approached Glasgow but the first coach was smashed to pieces and the next two were wrecked. There were a number of servicemen on the train who helped the casualties. Some Polish soldiers who had been on another train also came to help and used their field dressings to treat the injuries.

74. Naval men being issued with railway passes so they could go on leave. Troops were not only carried to war and back, but also when they went home on leave.

75. The memorial at Edinburgh's Waverly station to railway employees who died in both world wars. (*Linne Matthews*)

Thirty passengers had a lucky escape at Leeds when two coaches and the engine of a passenger train were derailed and turned on their sides after colliding with two petrol tanks and a guard's van. The petrol tanks and guard's van had become detached from a goods train and were burnt out by the collision. The thirty passengers on the passenger train were lucky to escape with cuts and bruises and none of them needed hospital treatment. The fireman of the passenger engine was thrown into the flames from the petrol tanks and was hospitalised with serious burns. The guard from the goods train, James Pearson, from Huddersfield, was killed. Reginald Briggs, a 17-year-old cleaner at the nearby locomotive sheds, ran along the passenger train opening carriage doors and giving first aid to injured passengers. He was then hit on the head by a door and taken to hospital for stitches. The driver of the passenger engine, Alan Mills, was still in the cab of the engine when it turned over. He ran along the line to place detonators and signal lamps to stop any oncoming trains.

In February, there was an even more serious accident at Beighton station, near Sheffield. A troop train ran into a piece of sheet steel that was projecting from a stationary goods train. The sides of the carriages were ripped open and soldiers and sailors were thrown on to the line. Miners and local villagers helped to drag the injured and the dead from the wreckage. Doctors and nurses arrived on the scene while some of the injured were taken to hospitals in Sheffield. The rescue work went on for four hours. The injured were mainly in the first part of the train. There were fourteen fatalities and thirty-six injured. Some of the men died on the way to hospital.

After the heavy bombing of the earlier years there had been plans for deep-level shelters to be built in London. These would be next to Tube stations – eight on the Northern Line and three on the Central Line. They were all to be connected with the Tube station they were next to but would have separate entrances with spiral staircases protected by blockhouses.

76. The Blockhouse, built as an entrance to the air raid shelter at Clapham South station. Some still survive in London. (*Kyra Foley*)

It was later decided that not all of them would be completed and no more would be planned, but by 1942, there were new shelters at Belsize Park, Camden Town, Goodge Street, Stockwell, Clapham North, Clapham Common, Clapham South and Chancery Lane. Many of the blockhouses still survive.

A number of railway projects were put on hold during the war. One of these was the Central Line extension out towards Epping. The tunnels were almost complete by the late 1930s but the war led to the cancellation of the new line for the period of the conflict. The tunnels, though, were to be put to use in another way. In 1940, the Plessey Company in Ilford was bombed. They were producing aircraft parts along with other war-related items. The company persuaded the Air Ministry and London Transport to let them utilise the unused Central Line tunnels between Leytonstone and Gants Hill as a wartime factory. The construction cost £500,000 and was completed by March 1942.

There were about 4,000 workers in the tunnels, mainly women. The entrances to the factory were through the unfinished stations at Wanstead, Redbridge and Gant Hill. Other shafts were installed to allow for deliveries to be made directly into the tunnels. At Redbridge, the line comes close to the surface and soil from the deep shelter construction in London was dumped there to protect the factory from bombs. Watertight doors were also fitted as it was close to the Roding River.

One employee who worked in the tunnels remembered that at Wanstead station there were two security men and passes had to be shown to enter. Although the Central Line wasn't working in the tunnels until after the war, there was a small mini railway installed to deliver goods and carry away finished products. The boss of Plessey, Nobby Clark, would use the light railway that had been built to ride through the tunnels. Tea was served during a ten-minute tea break by a man with two enamel buckets and a ladle. During the lunch break, many of the workers would come up and sit on the roundabout in the road at Gants Hill. The factory closed at the end of the war and the extension to the Central Line eventually opened in 1947.

There was a decision made about repairs to engines in April, when it was decided that as locomotives came up for repair they would all be painted black rather than keep their own company colours. No repainting could be done on carriages unless it was needed to protect them against bad weather. Interior decoration would only be updated if it helped the war effort.

An unexpected type of freight was being moved out of London in 1942. The bombing had led to great amounts of debris that had to be removed, but rather than being something that was of no use, it was regarded as an ideal form of building material. Places like the single branch line between Hadleigh and Ipswich had been very poorly used by both passengers and freight, although a few sidings had been added for trains carrying corn and sugar beet. Now, large amounts of the London debris were arriving on a line where the usual yearly total was about 400 tons; it was now nearer 57,000 tons. This wasn't the only quiet line in the area that was unexpectedly faced with enormous arrivals. The London debris was to be used for the foundations of the many airfields that were being built in East Anglia in the latter part of the war.

Consignments of tarmac and cement soon followed the arrival of the material for the foundations. Then came the large numbers of American servicemen, first to build the airfields and then to fly the aircraft that were going to bombard occupied Europe. Of the forty or so trains a day that the LNER were sending to East Anglia, fifteen of them were carrying fuel for the aircraft, which was pumped into large underground tanks.

London was still being subjected to air raids, along with many other places in Britain. York experienced a raid at the end of April involving about twenty German aircraft. As well as dropping their bombs, they also machine-gunned a cinema. It was reported that five of the raiders were destroyed. Some historic buildings were ruined but the Minster wasn't damaged. During the raid, the 10.15 pm LNER train from King's Cross to Edinburgh was machine-gunned and a nearby bomb explosion set fire to four of the carriages, which were then detached and left to burn. A number of passengers suffered burns and injuries from flying glass. Two railway staff died.

One of the passengers was Sir Eugene Ramsden, MP for North Bradford. He was in the vestibule between two sleeping carriages so was protected from the flying glass. He said that everyone on the train acted with courage and there was not the least tendency to panic. Help was efficiently and quickly administered to the injured.

Due to the government's efforts to dissuade people from travelling, a reduction of the passenger service by up to 50 per cent in the early years of the war seemed plausible. However, public demand for transport continued, with the need for workers to travel to and from work and servicemen to go back and forth between their homes and their units. This resulted in the reduced services becoming severely overcrowded. Although the number of passengers had initially shown a slight decrease, by 1942 they were back up to or even greater than pre-war figures. The railways were eventually forced to reduce passenger volume by 30 per cent rather than 50 per cent.

The public continued to defy government pleas for them not to travel. In March, local authorities were trying to stop evacuees from Tyneside returning home from the Lake District for Easter. Despite the opposition, the LMS provided a special train to take the evacuees home and also added extra coaches for them on scheduled trains.

The education authorities of Tyneside and Westmoreland had opposed the plan. The people of Westmoreland were annoyed as they had previously put on entertainments for the evacuees at holiday times. This was to encourage them to stay in the reception areas and not go home. Alderman Miss Jeffreys of the Kendal Education Committee argued that the children had been encouraged to leave the bombed areas and that going back was stupid, especially when the public had been asked not to travel.

One of the obvious areas to make cuts in traffic was on routes where the different rail companies had previously been in competition with each other. LMS took over passenger services to Glasgow, Perth and Inverness, and left Edinburgh, Dundee and Aberdeen to the LNER. The LNER also divided the times of trains to Birmingham with the GWR, who also ran trains to the city. Late night trains were also cut as they were mainly used by those travelling home from entertainment venues and not regarded as vital.

Getting workers to their jobs demanded greater planning, and as new factories opened producing war essentials, the number of workmen's trains actually increased. This was especially important when large armament factories were being built in remote areas and the only way for workers to get to them was by train.

Government directives for reduced public travelling would inevitably lead to fewer new passenger trains being needed, although orders for new engines were still being placed for war use. In addition, the government placed orders with the railway workshops for heavy military equipment as a factory that was designed to build railway locomotives could soon be adapted for the manufacture of heavy metal items like tanks and armour plating.

There had always been a tendency for the railway companies to buy in the heavier and clumsier products they needed, such as rails, from outside agencies. Their own workshops specialised more in the delicate work that necessitated long periods of experimentation. This meant that the workers had a great deal of experience in every kind of metalwork, which was an ideal basis for the production of precise military equipment.

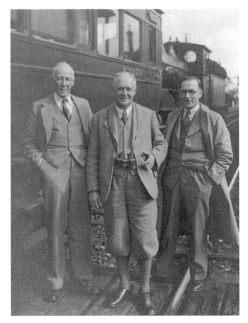

77. The railways provided services for affluent passengers before the war such as dining cars and sleepers. It was perhaps those affluent passengers who felt the changes more than most during wartime.

In many cases it was the design of military hardware that was carried out in the railway workshops and production took place elsewhere. The Covenanter tank was a prime example. There were thousands of drawings made at the Derby Works, along with numerous prints for component parts. The experiments often involved close co-operation with the military. There was even the creation of obstacle courses and artillery ranges for testing. For instance, a large amount of sand was imported into Derby when they were designing a tank to be used in the desert.

The workshops did, however, produce some military hardware that they had designed. There were thirty-five railway workshops involved in making weapons and munitions. Darlington produced a 2-inch naval rocket gun to combat dive-bombing at sea. York and Eastleigh were more involved with aircraft parts. Wings and bodies were made in the passenger coach departments. Often, railway workshops and outside producers would make a number of components between them before the finished article was assembled.

The anticipation that new railway equipment may not be needed as much during the war was unfounded. The widespread designation of railway workers making military hardware left less time and manpower for the fulfilment of railway production needs. To try to meet the demands for both military and railway equipment, the railway workshops were operating twenty-four hours a day, seven days a week. The employees were often working twelve hours a day without time off or holidays. There was no doubt that many of the workers, including women, were earning much more money than they ever had before but they had no time to spend it. Although workers were often sent to the workshops through the National Service scheme, they were not skilled in the jobs they were being sent to undertake. It was a skilled workforce that had made the railway workshops such an ideal place for the production of military hardware but this was now being watered down by inexperience.

Many of the workers were being sent to railway workshops against their will. These people did not make good employees; some proved impossible to train and were sent elsewhere. Even those who were keen to learn had to be trained by the skilled workers, which often stopped them from carrying out their own work.

There was, of course, a large increase in the number of women who were taken on in the workshops. Although there had been hardly any women outside of clerical workers on the railway before the war, it was soon found that many women could take on the strenuous manual work that was needed in the workshops – a fact that would have surprised many of the men there.

Women railway workers increased in number after the new National Service (Armed Forces) Act of November 1941, when unmarried women and childless widows aged 20 to 30 were called up to help solve the labour shortage. By 1942, the Act was adjusted to include women of 19 to 43 (50 for First World War veterans), and married women and men up to the age of 60. More nurseries were opened to provide childcare for those with children.

Eventually, there were young and old, married and unmarried women working on the railways, including girls just out of school and women with husbands serving overseas. Some of them were undertaking the heavy jobs in the workshops. Mrs Matthews worked in the finishing shop at Wolverton. She had a husband, son and granddaughter to look after at home but still managed to work six and a half hours a day helping the war effort. She was 62 when the war began and 67 when it ended.

The travelling public became used to seeing more women employed on the railways as booking clerks, ticket collectors and porters but were less aware of the roles that women were taking on in large goods depots, which were often operating twenty-four hours a day. At one large goods yard in London, of the 1,600 staff, 600 were women; they were driving cranes, loading and unloading goods, operating machinery and even working in the stables.

Women had first been employed in goods depots in March 1941, and the original plan had been that they would handle the lighter packages, but many had since volunteered for the heavier work. There were three women driving the 5-ton electric cranes and two of these were trained to drive the Goliaths – overhead cranes that could lift whole container trucks from trains straight on to lorries. Most of the women workers were married and in their twenties or thirties. Mrs Wenborn, who drove a 5-ton crane, was 25 years old and a former bakery shop manager. One of the crane drivers, Mrs Blackaby, worked 40 feet above the ground. She said that she was nervous of heights at first but had since come to like her job.

Women in the sheds worked in gangs, and a typical gang consisted of four women. One gang, for instance, comprised Mrs Day, a former tobacco shop manageress, Mrs Jones, who had worked in a laundry, and two others – a former milliner and one who had worked as a cook. Some female gang leaders were in charge of men in their gangs.

As well as working full time, many of the women also had homes and children to care for. Mrs Blackaby had two children at home. Stablewoman Mrs Owen started work at 5.00 am but also looked after two of her grandchildren when her daughter worked nights. Mrs Dearsley, in charge of the conveyor belt in a warehouse, was the mother of eleven – five at school, two in the forces and one working at the goods yard.

78. The GWR railway works at Swindon were thought to be the largest in the world. Staff were lucky enough to have a number of benefits for themselves and their families such as a medical service that was supposedly the inspiration for the National Health Service.

There was some conflict over new workers but this wasn't due to the difference in gender. The government orders tended to pay higher piecework rates than the old railway work. This often led to young girls earning more than skilled workers on the railway side of the line. To combat this there were attempts to move workers between railway and government work as long as it could be done without any loss of production.

The workshops in the south, at places like Brighton, Ashford and Lancing, had other problems to contend with. Ashford workshop was next to a junction and a marshalling yard, which became regular targets for German bombers, who could reach the site within seven minutes flying from France. At one point, large parts of the workshop had no roof due to bombing, but it was soon covered in tarpaulins.

The Times reported on 'Railways in War Time' and praised the railway system and its staff for performing an arduous task in an admirable and cheerful way. They commented that, by early in the year, this workforce included 40,000 women and not only were the staff good, but so were the locomotives – and the best of these were produced in Britain. This was down to years of excellent design and thorough workmanship – a reputation that had encouraged the government to place many military contracts with the railway workshops.

Following the close co-operation of railway companies during the First World War, between the wars they had forged agreements in aspects of day-to-day running, such as wages, fares, rates and charges. By this stage in the war, their co-operation was even greater. The diversion of freight and passenger trains from one company's lines to another was extensive. There had also been common use of wagons, whichever company they belonged to. Locomotives had been lent between companies to handle exceptional traffic. The use of locomotives on other company lines was shown by the daily leave train from Ashford to Newcastle, which began with a Southern engine as far as Banbury, where an LNER locomotive took over, which meant that no GWR engines had to get involved.

There were fifty-five Southern locomotives working on other company tracks. These included seventeen on the Somerset and Dorset joint line, twenty-four on the LMS, twelve on the GWR and two on the LNER. The LNER had a dock locomotive working on the LMS and twenty-eight freight engines on the GWS, who had lent the LMS forty freight engines.

There had been pre-war training for engine drivers for emergency working, and every locomotive shed on the LNER and the LMS had a list of enginemen who were ready to work over alternative routes. Also, when the LNER and the LMS were sending freight engines overseas they had to travel over unfamiliar dock railway lines that had curves, which were unsuitable for anything having a wheel base longer than that of a 10-ton wagon. Despite the occasional derailment, the engines usually reached their ships on time.

The quality of British workmanship was evident in the many older engines that were still in operation, some from the previous century – a fact that would be appreciated in the locomotives that had been sent overseas. Help was willingly given to allies such as Russia, despite the fact that the locomotives sent overseas could have been welcomed on to the overworked British system.

The strain on the railways was nowhere clearer shown than by the Schools class of engines on the Southern Railway, which were pulling sixteen or seventeen bogie coaches instead of the eleven that was usual in peacetime. The LNER express passenger's trains had increased from 450 to 650 tons. A King's Cross to Newcastle express pulled by the Pacific locomotive *Neil Gow* maintained its schedule pulling a load of 680 tons. A Green Arrow type mixed locomotive, No. 4800, pulled twenty-six vehicles that weighed more than 800 tons from Peterborough to London. Even this was surpassed by freight traffic from Midland collieries by the LMS, whose 153-ton sixteen-wheeled Garratt locomotives hauled mineral trains of eighty-six 13-ton wagons, which, including the brake van, weighed 1,400 tons.

In addition to locomotives pulling heavier trains, they also worked longer hours than they had in pre-war days. Many of the locos could cover over 100,000 miles between repairs. On the GWS, freight engines regularly recorded 1,200 to 1,500 miles from Monday to Friday, while LMS shunting diesels worked continuously for 144 hours each week.

The main task of Britain's railways during the war was, of course, keeping the system running at home. There was another aspect to their work and this was to provide the forces abroad with equipment and

79. Railway works being carried out at Totten, Hampshire.

goods. Great Western ships had played their part in the evacuation from Dunkirk but some troops also needed railway equipment.

British troops in Algeria were waiting for locomotives to arrive from Britain. They were hoping for the new Austerity 2-8-0 engines that had been built for the War Office, which would be able to cope with the steep African gradients. Unfortunately, these were not due to be introduced until 1943. What they got instead were Dean 0-6-0 locomotives from the Great Western. These had been designed by William Dean and produced in the late nineteenth century, and had been used by the military in the First World War. Despite their age they saw widespread use as far afield as France, Italy, North Africa and even China.

The railways were an important part in the chain of production of everything that was needed during the war. A report in *It Can Now be Revealed: More About British Railways in Peace and War*, published by the British Railways Press Office in 1945, gave a very good description of how the railways played a part in the setting up of a new factory. The factory described was an unnamed, large ordnance works in South Wales, although this has since been identified as the one built between the stations of Pencoed and Bridgend, in Mid Glamorgan. Although the factory had been planned at the outbreak of war it took three years before the building was completed. It was built on two sites alongside a main line of the GWS, which was a main reason for choosing the site. A deep underground magazine was built by digging into the hillside. This called for the supply of thousands of tons of building materials. The first items were carried by lorry from the railheads but then an internal line was built from the main line. This meant that wagonloads of materials were taken directly into the site. When building of the second site was undertaken nine months later, another line was laid to supply the materials. The cranes used to lift materials at the site were also supplied by the railway. The completed works contained 1,100 separate buildings covering 4 square miles, with 24 miles of rail track.

The building of the works was only the first step. There were more than 36,000 workers at the factory on three shifts. Most of these travelled to work by train to the four-platform station that was built for them at the site. Two signal boxes were also built to serve the lines. As well as carrying raw materials and workers to the factories, the railway also transported the manufactured armaments away.

80. A group of shunters – a dangerous job in wartime because of the blackout.

In Britain in 1942, there were still problems with coal supply due to it having to be unloaded by hand. Ernest Lemon had devised a system whereby domestic coal supplies could be stored in silos that could be tipped into rail wagons, making deliveries much faster, but the idea was never accepted by domestic coal suppliers.

The month of April was to see a new wave of air attacks by the Germans. These were known as the Baedeker raids and were thought to be in retaliation for RAF raids on Lübeck, an historic German town. The German targets were cultural and historic towns and cities in England.

One of these attacks was on York, when the station was hit. During the attack a streamlined Pacific locomotive, No. 4469, the *Sir Ralph Wedgewood*, named after a chief officer of the LNER who was also chairman of the Railway Executive Committee, was damaged. It was a relatively new loco, having been built at Doncaster in 1938. It was taken back to Doncaster for repair but was so badly damaged that it was later scrapped.

The bombing and shelling was still playing havoc at Dover Priory Street station. During one air raid in 1942, Mrs Clayton in the ticket office took shelter by lying on the floor and getting up to sell tickets to passengers when the danger seemed less acute, taking cover again when necessary. Although she escaped injury on this occasion she was later hurt by shelling and spent seven weeks in hospital. When a train arrived during an air raid, Mr Savage, the ticket collector, warned passengers to take shelter. One woman refused as she said she only had a short distance to go. When he came out of the shelter after the raid he found the woman dead.

Canterbury suffered many attacks and a total of 445 high explosive bombs fell on the city during the war. In June 1942 alone, 182 high explosive bombs and 8,000 incendiaries were dropped there. Railway staff and the military in the area had jointly received training in fighting fires.

An unusual move by the Railway Executive Committee came in August, when they decided that the London Passenger Transport Board had been correct in making some carriages on the Underground non-smoking. It was unusual in that smoking was so widespread at the time. The LPTB had published a notice stating that someone had been convicted for wilful refusal to observe the non-smoking rule in a no-smoking carriage. Only two out of seven were designated as no-smoking carriages. One lady, a Mrs Dyott Drayson, had protested against someone smoking in a non-smoking carriage. The lady was praised in a letter to *The Times* by The Reverend N.F. Duncan, who said that not a few smokers regarded the confined area of a railway carriage unsuitable for the indulgence of the habit. A good many timid passengers, however, preferred to suffer in silence … unlike Mrs Drayson.

The subject obviously caused a serious discussion on the matter, with a further letter in *The Times* from Mr J. Wardale who said that he agreed with Mrs Drayson but would hesitate to request that someone in an American or Canadian uniform should comply with the no-smoking rule. Mr F.H. Bessemer, however, had an opposing view and said in his letter that non-smokers should not travel in a smoking compartment. Mr G.F. Moorman went even further and claimed that smoking was almost a universal habit and that while trains were painfully crowded with fighting men and women, he suggested that the necessarily restricted public travelling facilities should not allow the distinction between smoking and non-smoking.

Despite the widespread bombing, not all railway staff felt themselves to be in danger. When Maud Fricker began work as a porter on the Southern, she was more concerned about how heavy the task of unloading trains was. She worked in a gang of women and they were paid according to the weight of what they unloaded. She said that women worked together and the men worked together. Maud was later promoted to working on a barrow as a proper porter, which was better money as she was paid by the hour. She was also given a uniform with trousers, which were much more convenient than a skirt.

The women had to work Monday to Friday, and Saturday mornings. If they had to work on a Saturday afternoon or Sunday, they were paid overtime. Maud didn't remember ever having any holidays. They had a room where they could eat their lunch if they brought their own. The only danger she remembered was being in a shelter during a raid and hearing popping noises when a fire bomb had made a load of lemonade bottles explode.

There was an unusual type of damage caused at York in September when a fitter's mate drove a pilot engine into the rear of a 98-ton locomotive and pushed it towards a pit 13 feet deep. Albert Groves was seen driving the engine by Mr C.E. Tilley, the assistant divisional locomotive superintendent. He said that Groves refused to leave the footplate, reversed the engine and said that he was going to have another go at it.

Groves was aggrieved because the railway company would not release him to take up another job that he had found. This was despite his work

81. Engine No. 9022, built at Swindon, pulling a freight train at Whitechurch.

for the company not being a reserved occupation. He drove the engine into the other locomotive hoping that he would be dismissed. He had made sure that the wheels of the locomotive were locked so he would not do much damage. Groves was not dismissed but was sentenced to three months in prison on a charge of committing an act with intent to impair the efficiency of a vehicle used in essential service.

In Eastbourne, on 16 September, there was a demonstration of fire pumps by the inspector of railway staff. The demonstration was hit by a bomb, which destroyed the pumps and killed the inspector and some of the staff.

In October, there was an appeal to employers to try to make changes to what was obviously a rush hour on London's trains. Quarter past five was the most crowded time on London's transport system as most offices in the capital finished work at five o'clock. It was estimated that 35,000 people entered the central area of the Underground in those fifteen minutes. In the fifteen minutes before this, the number was 20,000, and in the fifteen minutes after, 24,000. These figures don't include those travelling on the bus routes.

The same thing happened in the morning in the period between 8.45 am and 9.15. There were about 26,000 people in each fifteen-minute period leaving the central Underground. Between 9.45 and ten o'clock, the numbers were nearer 12,000. There were calls for offices to stagger their starting and finishing times to avoid the rush.

There was also a request that schools start their day later as many of those travelling during the busy period before nine o'clock were children making their way to school. Industrial establishments were already staggering their starting and finishing times, as were some schools, but more could obviously be done. Many of the offices in London causing the problem were government departments.

It wasn't only large towns and cities that suffered from attacks. Templecombe in Somerset – a small village whose population at the time were almost all connected with the railway – was bombed in October and thirteen people died, five of whom were railway employees.

A letter sent to *The Times* by Mr G. Cole Deacon, Secretary of the Railway Executive, makes very interesting reading in relation to the importance of war-related goods and how the railways were struggling to cope with the increased load. He stated that from January to June 1942, cut flowers from principal growing areas to the main markets carried by train totalled 9,000 tons. This meant that 8,000 trucks were used, some attached to normal passenger trains, but there had also been 365 special flower trains. This seems a strange fact considering that the railway companies had cut some fish trains. This was due to the Ministry of Food's fish distribution scheme, which had come into operation the previous year to cut out the middlemen who would get to the market early to cash in on gluts, which in wartime served no purpose, and who may even have been involved in black market activities. Not everyone was in agreement with the scheme. Mr John Adamson, director of the fish division of the Ministry of Food, said that he had seen a notice in a fishmonger's shop that said: Fish Zoning Scheme, no fish. The fish industry's joint council had claimed that the scheme was likely to lead to a complete breakdown of distribution.

In October, the Eighth Railway Company RE arrived from Northern Ireland at Melbourne Military Railway. The company occupied most of the Melbourne and Ashby-de-la-Zouch branch line, which had closed to passengers in the 1930s. The Melbourne training centre had been opened earlier in the war because it was thought that Longmoor did not have enough capacity to train all the railwaymen that would be needed in France.

The site at Melbourne had few of its own railway vehicles, although when the American Army 0-6-0 tanks began to arrive in Britain, many of them went to Longmoor and Melbourne. They were painted dark grey with USA and WD lettering. The Eighth Company later moved again to Longmoor.

The advantages of control systems during wartimes had proved to be of great value. The ability to arrange the working of areas hour by hour according to the circumstances was a way of overcoming unforeseen events such as air raids and keeping things running smoothly. This was especially true of the railway system.

Before the war, there had been a telephone control system on the railway but this had been greatly improved during the conflict. The system now enabled centralisation of control offices and the supervision of working traffic. This led to the better loading of trains, an increase in the miles travelled and a reduction in trains running empty. Line capacity had been improved by the system in a manner very similar to military organisation. In cases of emergency it was much easier to divert traffic to alternative routes in unaffected areas. It also meant that signal boxes, stationmasters, yardmasters and foremen had access to control rooms at all times.

On 16 December, the Guildford to Horsham train was attacked by bombing and machine-gun fire from a Dornier aircraft near Bromley. The guard and the driver both died in spite of the efforts of six Canadian soldiers to save them. There had only been twenty passengers on the train but eight of these also died.

There had been a great change in rail travel for passengers during the war and the 1942 passenger figures show this clearly. Mainline rail travel during the year totalled 30 billion miles (or '30,000 million', as reported in *British*

Day in - day out . . . . . Night in - night out

BRITISH RAILWAYS operate 20,000

British built LOCOMOTIVES in the

service of NATION and PUBLIC!

BRITISH RAILWAYS ARE CARRYING ON

82. Another wartime railway advertisement that describes how British Rail were carrying on, without mentioning any of the Big Four or the Railway Executive Committee.

Railways in Peace and War). This was a 50 per cent increase on pre-war figures. At the same time, there was a reduction of 28 per cent in the mileage run by passenger trains. This indicated that the loading of the trains had more than doubled.

Locomotives had to spend more time at work than they did in peacetime. They spent 11 per cent more time in use, while the number of available locomotives increased by less than 1 per cent.

From the outbreak of war to the end of 1942, 587 locomotives were built by railway workshops and another fifty were supplied from outside contractors. To ensure that there was a pool of locomotives that could also be used overseas it had been decided that all new heavy locomotives

83. The wagon-building shed and sawmill at Swindon. Production was more concerned with wartime goods than domestic railway items.

should be built to one design. The LMS 2-8-0 type was selected as the standard. These were ideal for more general use. There were some other new designs for freight and mixed traffic locomotives, with each company producing their own. These were the Southern 4-6-2 Merchant Navy mixed traffic, the Austerity 0-6-0 freight class, the LNER 4-6-0 two-cylinder mixed traffic class and 0-8-0 shunting engines.

According to *The Times*, it was planned that by the end of the year, khaki-coloured engines would be running on the railway system. They were part of an order placed by the War Office. The engines would not have names but would have the letters WD and a number. The locomotives were designed for hauling munitions and troops. They were standard gauge and fitted with vacuum brake equipment or the Westinghouse system, and also had a steam brake on the engine. They could be used anywhere in the world that had a standard gauge railway.

The engines were described as Austerity locomotives; all embellishments were sacrificed and the design simplified to the bare requirements of utility. This resulted in a large saving of materials that were in short supply, and also of man hours in construction. The steel casing in a normal engine would weigh 21 tons, and in the utility engine weighed 4 tons. They would take 6,000 man hours less to build so that five could be built in the same time that it took four normal locomotives to be built.

They had large tenders because when operating abroad, there was a chance that fuel and water may be in short supply. Able to draw a load of 500 to 700 tons, they had a maximum speed of 30 to 40 miles an hour. Engines were in demand all over the world, and Britain and the USA were combining their resources to meet the demand. There had originally been plans to build forty engines a month but the rapid fall of France led to the building of tanks being made a priority.

The Austerity engines were used in Britain before being sent abroad, where they were renumbered to avoid confusion with engines already in the country that they had been sent to. There were a number of different designs for the Austerity engines. However, although *The Times* said that there were plans for the engines to be completed by the end of the year, Austerity engines of various designs had been in production since 1940.

New engines were urgently needed as a large number of trains were being cancelled due to shortages of locomotives, at a time when the

84. Mr Albert Taylor being presented with a gold medal by the mayor of Weston-super-Mare, Alderman Henry Butt, at the Weston-super-Mare GWR ambulance class at Brown's café. Ambulance services were, of course, utilised heavily during the war.

amount of freight and passenger traffic was increasing due to the war. Not only was there a shortage of locomotives, but hundreds of those still in use were so old that they would have been scrapped in peacetime.

At the military railway training camp at Longmoor there were some new arrivals towards the end of the year. These were the American Army 0-6-0 tanks, which had small alterations made to their engines at Longmoor. There was also an old LMS 0-6-0 tank, which had been built at Crewe in 1878. It had been dismantled and was used for training.

The boiler was used to practise renewing stays and changing boiler tubes. To do this the trainee had to climb in through the firehole. When one man tried to climb in he found that he couldn't fit through the hole. Perhaps this was a job best fit for younger, thinner trainees. There was even a report of a pregnant women being caught in a firehole in one of the railway workshops.

Chapter 7

1943

The production of Austerity engines was still going on into 1943. The Austerity 2-8-0 was designed by Robert Arthur 'Robin' Riddles, who had designed other Austerity engines, and it was the most numerous locomotive built for use on the Western Front. From 1943, nearly 1,000 were built by the North British Loco Company, Glasgow, and the Vulcan Foundry, Newton-le-Willows, Lancashire. They were based on the LMS 2-8-0 class 8F engines and many of the parts were interchangeable with the LMS type. Numbers 7000 to 7049 were built by the North British Locomotive Company in 1943, and Nos. 7050 to 7149 by the Vulcan Foundry in the same year.

The Beyer Garratt 4-8-2 and 2-8-4 were started in 1942 but wartime production carried on into 1943 and later. These were a metre gauge and were the largest and most powerful locomotives working on that gauge.

The Austerity 0-6-0 ST locomotive was one of the most numerous of the Austerity engines built. It was designed by the Hunslet Engine Company, Leeds, and built from 1943 to 1945 by six private companies, including Hunslet. The other companies were Stephenson, Hudswell Clarke, Barclay, Bagnall, and Vulcan. They were well represented in army depots and dock areas at home and in much of Europe.

Pilfering was still a severe problem at this time. At Manchester Quarter Sessions in January 1943, Ambrose Rayson, a parcels porter from Cheetham, pleaded guilty to stealing parcels containing 120 pairs of stockings, two fur coats and a quantity of clothing valued at more than £160 from the LMS Railway at London Road station, Manchester. The thefts took place between July and December the previous year. The prosecution alleged that Rayson took the parcels and readdressed them to a friend, Cecil Carter, at Woodland's Road station, labelled 'To be called for'. Carter was an aircraft fitter and claimed that he was told by Rayson that he was a general dealer. He had no idea that Rayson was a railway porter or that the goods were stolen. Carter was found not guilty and Rayson was sent to prison for nine months.

There was a serious threat to the smooth running of the railways as the new year began. The railway enginemen's trade union, ASLEF, were warning the government that within the next two weeks there could be a strike if their demands were not met. The enginemen had received the same rise in wages as the rest of the railway staff but in their eyes this led to a loss of financial status, which they believed to be their right as they saw themselves as superior to other rail workers.

Representations were to be made to the Minister of Labour and National Service, Ernest Bevin, and the Minister of War Transport, Lord Leathers. The enginemen were arguing that the increase in wages had not been consistent with advances made to other grades or the importance of their work. It seemed as if the enginemen's position was not supported by their fellow workers. Mr Marchbank, the General Secretary of the National Union of Railwaymen (NUR) had denounced talk of a strike as 'pure irresponsibility'.

The docks were playing a vital role in the war effort. This was shown in advertisements published in the national press. One of these had the words 'Thanks, sailor! YOU CAN LEAVE IT TO THE RAILWAYS NOW', and showed a ship with a train alongside it. It was also interesting that the words

Thanks, Sailor!
YOU CAN LEAVE IT TO THE RAILWAYS NOW -

EVERY week, every day, every hour almost, ships of all kinds and sizes are bringing vital supplies to these shores on the first stage of their journey to supplement Britain's war effort.

The next and no less complex stage is left to the railways. It is their task to convey and distribute millions of tons of freight to thousands of destinations—urgent, material for the war factories; food and equipment for the troops; guns and tanks and aeroplanes and the ever-growing personnel of Dominion and American Armies.

The railways carry these vast and valuable burdens safely and efficiently despite the fact that they have released more than 100,000 skilled workers for the forces, and have sent overseas many locomotives and thousands of railway wagons.

BRITISH RAILWAYS
GWR · LMS   LNER · SR

Carrying the War Load

85. An advertisement publicising how the railways carried goods brought in by ship. This one mentions British Railways and the Big Four.

'BRITISH RAILWAYS' were displayed twice as large as the initials of the Big Four in the advertisement.

Despite the advertisement, the docks were obviously vital, but some played a larger role than others. Plymouth harbour's wartime role was mainly naval and much of the town had grown to serve the Admiralty dockyards. These were mainly on the western side. There were also two large commercial basins on the south shore at Millbank that were owned by the GWR. The private wharfs on the east, on the Cattewater estuary, were privately owned but connected to the SR, which also owned its own wharfs at Stonehouse Pool.

Plymouth docks had a sporadic connection to London throughout the war. Sometimes the Admiralty closed the docks for a few days a week but most of the traffic comprised small ships. The size of the freight using Plymouth had declined in the war years up to 1943.

Much of the traffic going out of the harbour was scrap iron from the destruction caused by bombing and was being sent to other British harbours. There was also an increase in naval and military traffic now that D-Day was on the horizon. One of the new imports was American soldiers and airmen, and also the food and supplies to feed them. Many of the convoys crossing the Atlantic arrived at ports in the west of the country, including Plymouth.

There was a great change in the carrying of freight during the war. Before the war, a company such as the LNER or the LMS carrying freight from somewhere in the north and going to the south would take it to London before passing it on to another company to continue its journey. This was because the company would be paid for the distance it carried the freight, so would keep it as long as it could. During the war, there was no financial gain by working in this way so it was more conducive to keeping the goods moving and getting them to their final destination by transferring them to other companies' routes in the Midlands, from where they could travel a more direct route to delivery. The new system also helped to reduce the traffic through London, which was under greater threat of attack than other areas.

The carrying of freight could go in cycles. The convoy system of ships protected by the navy had been in action since the war began. This meant that supply ships no longer arrived in the country in an even flow. They

86. Two engines in a roofless shed at Tilbury. The docks were active throughout the war, and boats left from there for Dunkirk. The docks were heavily bombed and were also the site of a large army camp just before D-Day, from where many of the men left for Normandy.

came in waves as the men of war were available to escort them, and they came in large numbers, all at once.

Their arrival was often kept secret to avoid enemy activity, which made it difficult for the men working at the ports and the railwaymen who had to move the goods without knowing when they would arrive. The ships had to be unloaded and then reloaded and turned around to wait for the return voyage as quickly as possible. This also included the naval ships that were to escort them on the return journey. This resulted in periods of intense activity, with cranes operating night and day.

The docks themselves were often not able to cope with sudden influxes, and warehouses were crammed to the roofs. There was a saying on the railway that the ship can always beat the quay. This meant that the ship could be unloaded much quicker than the goods could be sorted and distributed into railway trucks. The delay could only be reduced as long as there were enough trains waiting to remove the goods. The fact that only a few ports were taking in goods made the problem even more difficult to deal with. The short notice of arrivals meant that it was always problematic to get the right number and type of trucks to the docks quickly enough. The trains then had to move off to numerous destinations through the normal traffic on main lines and branch lines throughout the country.

The type of engines used varied according to need. There were numerous types of wheel arrangement, which had little to do with age. Many of the engines in use at docks were 0-4-0, although shunters were more commonly 0-6-0. For long-distance expresses the more common arrangement was 4-6-2 with a leading pivoted bogie, which meant a shorter, rigid wheel base and a pair of small wheels behind the driver. There were company variations, however, as the GWR preferred a 4-6-0. This was mainly due to the long, straight level roads out of London on the company's routes. The company also developed automatic train control signalling and was one of the leaders in fast trains. Until the war, the GWR was also able to rely on very high-quality coal from South Wales. This generated high levels of heat, which meant that their locomotives needed smaller fireboxes and so did not need the wheels at the back of the engine.

The LMS was also close to South Wales and could obtain supplies of the same coal. They had a number of 4-6-0 locomotives, some of which were designed by an engineer who had worked on the GWR. The LNER built big engines, which were 4-6-2s. Their Pacifics were both streamlined and non-streamlined. The company also had some 4-6-0s and 4-4-0s as their express runs tended to be over shorter distances.

* * *

One of the worst tragedies to strike on the London Underground during the war occurred on 3 March 1943. There had been heavy Allied bombing of Germany, and Londoners feared a reprisal. When the air raid sirens started during the evening, crowds of people made their way towards Bethnal Green station. The station was to be part of the Central Line extension begun in the 1930s but was being left unused until after the war, although it was being used as an air raid shelter.

As well as those making their way to the station on foot, buses were disgorging passengers at the station entrance and they began to make their way down the narrow, poorly lit entrance. In nearby Victoria Park, the sound of new anti-aircraft rockets being fired panicked the crowd into thinking they were bombs. At the bottom of the stairs someone fell and tripped up others who were coming behind. The rest of the people trying to reach the shelter carried on pushing into the narrow entrance. There were no officials or police on site to try to control the crowd.

Finally, air raid wardens and an off-duty police officer arrived and began to hold back the crowd, but it was too late for those at the bottom. In the horrendous crush, twenty-seven men, eighty-four women and sixty-two children died. The youngest, Carol Geary, was five months old. There were also a number of injured who were at the top of the crush. One of the survivors, Alf Morris, was pulled out by an ARP warden, Mrs Chumley. Alf's guardian, his Aunt Lil, was the last survivor to be pulled out.

The official version of what happened was that the station had suffered a direct hit by an enemy bomb, but in reality, no bombs had dropped that night. A *Daily Mail* reporter had been a witness, but his truthful version of events was censored. After the tragedy the station was updated with a central handrail, better lighting and toilets, as well as bunk beds for those sheltering there.

The blackout was causing a number of accidents on the railways as well as in other walks of life. Luckily for one passenger on the LMS, a railway guard was on the alert and put his own life at risk to save him. The passenger had changed places on the train during his journey and seemed to have lost all sense of direction in the dark. As the train reached a station, the passenger stepped out of the wrong side of the train and fell on to the tracks. The guard, Mr Ernest George Chandler, heard a shout and saw the passenger standing on the rails as another train approached. Chandler jumped on to the rails and pulled the man in-between two of the carriages of the stationary train. Mr Chandler was awarded the British Empire Medal for his promptitude and coolness.

The duties of a train driver were often underestimated and went beyond just driving. He carried out some duties before he even reached the footplate. When checking on for duty, a driver had to read the noticeboard, and any notices had to be signed for. There were often important points included, such as the shutting off of water supplies at

87. The memorial in the park outside Bethnal Green station. The disaster was described as a direct hit during the war but was in fact caused by people being crushed on the stairs while trying to get into the station to shelter from what they thought was a bomb attack.

some points, and details of engineering and signal work. Running times and stopping places had to be looked up. Only then would the driver go and find out which engine he would be driving. Then the water level had to be checked, the gauges tested and steam pressure recorded. The coal level was inspected and the firebox examined, and the engine needed to be checked while being oiled.

Although drivers were obviously an important part of the railway system, there were many other workers who were also seen as important. This was shown when Watton House, near Hertford, once the home of the late Sir Nigel Gresley, Chief Mechanical Engineer of the LNER, was opened as a training school for station clerks. The school took twenty trainees at a time on a residential basis.

Most of the clerical staff at stations were women so the trainees at the school were all female. The school was opened by Mr C.H. Newton, Chief General Manager of the LNER. Training schools for clerks were not a new idea; in fact, this was the third one opened by the LNER. The others were at Whitley Bay and Scarborough, and based in dining cars in the stations, while the pupils slept in nearby boarding houses.

There were almost 100,000 women working on the railways by this time, but most of them were not clerks. It must have been embarrassing for men to get off a train and find a female porter waiting to carry their cases. The ladies took up jobs that were often far removed from their previous occupation. One music teacher, for example, became a blacksmith in a railway shop. Women working in such jobs were trendsetters in fashion; before the war it had been rare to see women in trousers.

By now it had become evident that women could manage to do many of the jobs that had previously been considered 'men's work'. The Southern Railway had opened two schools for female guards, at Victoria and Brighton, and the LMS had trained a hundred women to drive lorries and platform tractors.

There was one area in which many women did not do as well as men – and that was in wages. By the end of the war, many women on the railways were earning up to four pounds a week, but men doing the same work earned more. Women in government training centres were paid around a third less than their male colleagues in the same jobs. The railway companies were challenged by the unions to pay women the same as men, despite not many women having joined the unions. The company argued that they had not been able to find any industry where equal pay for equal work was applied, so why should the railways do so?

On 24 March, the electrical workshop at Ashford, Kent, was bombed and a quarter of the shop was destroyed. Eight people died and forty-one were injured. An area around the works was also badly damaged and dozens were killed.

Government attempts to dissuade the public from travelling were continuing. Up until this point they had not been very successful. A new catchword was brought in as the holiday period approached, with the government trying to make it a 'no travel Easter'. Train times were published in the national press for the Easter period. Good Friday had weekday services, and Saturday had a normal Saturday service with the cancellation of workmen's trains, which were not needed. There was a Sunday service on Easter Sunday and a Saturday service on Easter

Monday. On the London Underground, Sunday services were run over the Easter weekend apart from Good Friday, which was a normal weekday service.

There was also an attempt to stop those who wanted to watch trains being able to make a record of what they had seen. It was against the law to photograph railways or trains as they were playing an important role in the war effort. The interest in trains did not stop for those who had been watching them before the war. There was an exhibition of photographs of railway locomotives arranged by British Rail and London Transport in the offices of Dean and Dawson Limited, of 81 Piccadilly, London. The display had seven sections: Once Upon a Time; The Gay Nineties; Early Days of the Live Rail; Express Passenger; Heavy Freight; The Streamlined Era; and Electrics and Diesels Grow Up. The exhibition showed the evolution of the railways in Britain up until the war.

Information about the railways appeared in the press and in April, a reporter from *The Times* accompanied an engineering team working on the London Underground during the night. He said that he doubted if passengers gave a thought to how they were kept safe on the 200 miles of tracks on the system. There were 500 workers, mainly men, but also a few women who worked in gangs cleaning and repairing the Underground during the night. The permanent way (the rails and sleepers) needed to be inspected every night, with rails taken up and renewed, sleepers refastened and bolts tightened.

The gang the reporter worked with descended 360 steps, so it must have been one of the deep stations. They passed members of the public asleep in bunks in the station. The reporter was surprised to see the normally dark tunnels lit during the night by electric lamps. The 60-foot lengths of rail, each weighing 17 hundredweight, were handled with a chain tackle slung over the bolts. Before this was done the power had to be switched off. The power was not switched on again until written permission was given by the ganger confirming that all his men were off the line. A gang of twenty-six men could take up and renew 320 yards of track in two and a half hours.

There was a women's gang working in the original tunnel built by Brunel in 1843, which was still used by trains running under the Thames. Their job was to clean the tracks, which were caked with fluff and brake dust. The women, known as 'fluffers', worked in pairs collecting the dust into containers, and these were then removed by a special train. When they got home they had housework and shopping to do before they could go to bed at lunchtime. Some had small children to get to bed before they went back to work the next night.

Overcrowded trains, especially during the rush hour, were a source of danger for the passengers. This was shown in April, when a rush-hour train crashed at Victoria. It was the 7.12 am from Tunbridge Wells and it collided with the buffers on platform seventeen. Thirty-three men and fifteen women were treated at St George's Hospital, where six men were detained. The Southern Railway, whose train it was, said that there was a slight telescoping of the first coach. They estimated that there were eight stretcher cases and forty cases of slight injury and shock. A considerable proportion of the casualties were due to passengers having to stand during their journey, with the result that they were thrown down.

A conference in London in May examined the efficiency of the use of coal. It was opened by the Minister of Fuel and Power, Major Gwilym Lloyd George. Major George described coal as not merely *a* munition of war, but *the* munition of war, as without it the mobilisation of the armed forces and labour for industry would be impossible. Even work of the highest priority did not carry a licence to waste coal. The conference was told of the importance of fuel watchers and Major George would not be satisfied until every industry, however small, had a fuel watcher. The regional fuel efficiency inspectors had at that point only managed to examine about 17 per cent of the country's industries. Mr M.G. Bennet referred to economies in the use of coal on the railways. This had been achieved by shortening the period when train carriages were heated by five weeks. In the locomotive works, two of the most effective economy methods had involved repairs to insulation, and air recuperation by the use of waste heat to warm incoming air. This had led to savings of 10 to 40 per cent of coal.

The dedication of railway staff was shown when, in May, there was a parade of 2,000 LMS railway Home Guards of East Lanarkshire and Derbyshire at Belle Vue, Manchester. Many of the men had been working all night until six o'clock that morning, but still made it to the parade. A number of them arrived by train at Victoria station, where they were

88. The Home Guard took over the job of guarding the railways from the regular army. There were a number of units of the Home Guard that were railway employees.

joined by men serving in the Manchester battalions. The men assembled in the grounds of the Chetham's Hospital and then marched to Belle Vue. They were led by the band of the 50th Lancashire Battalion and were inspected by Colonel G.S. Hussey, group commander of the LMS Home Guard London.

Although some express trains had been stopped during the war there was a shortage of trains on the LNER London to Edinburgh route, which was used by a large number of military personnel. To combat this, in June, a midday express in each direction was restored. They also decided to run two nightly trains all week except Saturday; they had previously only been run on a Friday.

From 3 July 1940 to 4 September 1943, there were fifty-eight attacks on trains on the Southern Railway area, most of which took place in the daytime. On 25 May, the railway viaduct in Brighton between the town and London Road was bombed, destroying one of the central brick piers while leaving the metal reinforcements standing. There was also severe damage to the railway workshops and rolling stock.

Apart from air raids, travelling on the railways during the war seems to have been very safe. The annual report of the Chief Inspecting Officer of Railways in July showed that there had been remarkably few accidents of a serious nature in the previous year. This was notwithstanding an increase of 20 per cent in passengers compared with 1941.

The forty-six deaths among passengers, railway servants and other persons in the past year compared to an average thirty-nine a year in the five-year period of 1935–39. Twenty-eight of the fatalities in the previous year had occurred in two accidents. This meant that the chance of a passenger being killed was one in 60 million.

There had been 547 accidents in 1942, and 233 of these had been caused by human failure. In accidents connected with the movement of railway vehicles exclusive of train accidents, 113 passengers were killed compared with an average of sixty-eight in the years 1935–39. Of these, eighty-three were caused by falling from platforms or trains, or when entering or alighting from trains, compared with eighty-one in 1941. The blackout was given as a cause in twenty-four deaths, although fifty-eight occurred during the blackout; the others were largely due to misadventure or a lack of caution by the passengers. The number of women employees on the railways was by this time about 100,000, but only four women had been killed in accidents in 1942.

There were reports that many of the women who took jobs on the railway did not bother to join a union. Some obviously did, however, as at the NUR conference at Carlisle in July, Mr T. Gibson, a Glasgow ticket collector, said that women who had become members of the NUR often showed more interest in their trade union than men did. He went on to say that the women were also anxious to see that they were not endangering the positions of male workers. Conference delegates praised the hard work – cheerfully carried out – of women on the railways. They then demanded that the principle of equal pay for similar work be applied throughout the railway service. The Assistant General Secretary, Mr W.J. Watson, complained that many women clerks undertook the same duties as men at less pay and that the railway companies were deliberately exploiting the war situation to employ more women clerks.

The use of trains to combat any invasion threat had been in operation for much of the war. The railway works at Ashford in Kent had produced armoured trains. There were four of these in the Southern area, at Tonbridge, Barnstable, Canterbury and Wadebridge. They included a tank engine with runner wagons on each side and 20-ton armoured trucks at each end. They were armed with anti-aircraft guns, another gun and anti-grenade nets. The drivers of the armoured trains were from a military operating unit. The trains were also to be rallying points for the Home Guard. They were used to patrol their areas, travelling at 25 miles an hour, until 1943, when the danger of invasion was thought to have declined.

The railway had their own Home Guard detachments, and O Company of the 6th Battalion Worcestershire Regiment were Great Western men. In July, they paraded in the station drive at Kidderminster under the command of Major W. Smith, who was a company officer. They were inspected at Paddington by Colonel K.W.C. Grand, Assistant General Manager of the GWR, who was liaison officer to the railway company's Home Guard units. He congratulated the men on their smart turnout and said that they obviously realised the seriousness of the job they were doing after their normal working hours.

Many of the Home Guard units were made up of railwaymen; there were twenty-five battalions that were exclusively made up of railwaymen. It was hoped that these would be a special force for railway defence. This was closest to happening in the Southern area, where the railway Home Guard units were under separate control, but in most other areas the railway units became part of the regular Home Guard units.

The majority of the men in the Home Guard never saw any action as their main objective was to take part in defending against invasion. Some units did, however, take charge of anti-aircraft batteries near stations and docks, usually where the members were working. This was so that they could man the guns at a moment's notice. These were the only Home Guard units to see action.

The continuing appeals of the government to deter the public from travelling were still not being met and on the last weekend of July 1943, this was shown when the greatest 'holidays from home' rush since the war began took place. Masses of travellers jammed the platforms and barriers at London railway stations over the weekend. The stations were so busy that many people were waiting in the streets to get in. At

89. The war memorial inside the entrance to King's Cross station. It lists all the names of the railway employees of the Great Northern Railway killed in the First World War. It was further dedicated to employees of the LNER who lost their lives in the Second World War, but they are not individually named.

midnight, there were 2,000 people at Waterloo station who could not get on a train going to the West Country. Many of these spent the night there waiting for the next day's trains. Racegoers heading for Salisbury were also caught in the rush at Waterloo, and some officials did not arrive until after the first race. Manchester had its biggest holiday crowds of the war so far. It was estimated that at least 150,000 people reached Blackpool on the Saturday, and many thousands left for Welsh holiday resorts. The government were still asking people not to travel by train in the following weeks, and especially to stay off the trains on the Bank Holiday weekend in August as no extra passenger trains would run then.

There had been an increase in traffic as preparations for the invasion of Europe had already begun in 1943. This was an obvious reason for the government to try to deter the public from taking unnecessary journeys by train. The request for people not to travel on August Bank holiday was also partly driven by the fact that the Minister of Agriculture had estimated the harvest that year would amount to 100 million tons of food. The area of land under cultivation had increased by about 7 million acres since 1939. This had already presented the railways with more work in distributing fertilisers and seeds, along with farm machinery, and now the railways were expected to carry the harvest.

The railways were required to transport the largest amount of grain they had ever had to carry – a 12½ per cent increase on the previous year. Home-grown grain was more perishable than imported grain and needed careful collection and transport. Once the grain harvest was finished then the transport of sugar beet would begin. The sugar beet factory at Foley Park, Kidderminster, had trainloads of beet delivered during a season that lasted from mid-September to mid-January. The trains carrying the beet came from as far away as the West Country and Pembrokeshire, so they were pulled by a variety of locomotives, with sometimes as many as four trains a day arriving at Kidderminster. During the season there were two shunting engines needed to transfer the trucks to the factory. The beet supplied 30 per cent of the country's sugar needs. Members of the Women's Institute used it to make jam for the war effort.

The LMS had begun to provide refreshment bars at several of their stations and these were supplied by train. Now the passengers could buy snacks to take on the trains with them. There were two types of refreshment bars. The first was a permanent structure, at Euston. Since it opened, 900,000 passengers had used its facilities. The second type was for non-terminal stations; these were temporary and could be erected quickly without interfering with rail traffic, and could be run with a minimum of staff. These were opened at Crewe, Preston, Derby, Sheffield and Rugby.

There had been attempts to improve lighting on the railways as, by now, the number of air raids had declined, but there had been difficulty in achieving this on the Southern Railway, where the theft of light bulbs and damage to fittings was an increasing problem. In the previous six months on Southern alone, each month there had been more than 7,000 special shades and 12,000 light bulbs stolen. There were also 500 blinds taken and over 2,000 damaged every month. In Scotland, during the first six months of the year, the LMS lost 16,300 light bulbs, and 2,200 blackout shades stolen or damaged. The position on the LNER was similar; thefts had been very heavy on the suburban lines from Liverpool Street. The GWR also recorded large losses of blinds, shades and bulbs. Special measures were taken by the police and in forty-six prosecutions, fines of up to £5 were handed down, with three guineas' costs. The railways had asked passengers to help them provide a better service by reporting anyone seen interfering with lights or blackout equipment.

The year 1943 saw the beginnings of preparations for the invasion of Europe to take place the following year. Miles of new sidings were built and 72 miles of pipes for oil were laid from Walton-on-Thames to Lydd, which was the site of an artillery firing range. The transfer of oil was also happening in other places and in the Essex marshes there was an old railway being used for that purpose.

There had been a munitions works called Kynoch's on Canvey Island during the First World War. As well as the works, there had also been a village known as Kynochtown. After the war, the works closed and the whole area was sold to Cory Brothers Ltd. in 1921. Although this also included the light railway that ran to the works from Corringham, there was always some dispute about who owned it. The Corringham Light Railway had been built in 1898 and was one of the smallest in the country at 3 miles in length. It had no signals and was mainly independent for its lifetime. Cory Brothers Ltd. had strong railway connections. They had owned a network of coal depots and a fleet of more than 5,000 railway wagons and coal trucks. They built an oil depot on the site, and tankers came in on the Thames and oil was transferred to the light railway. When the deliveries of oil moved to the west coast, they stored vegetable oil for the Ministry of Food. The railway was also used to move goods for the build-up to D-Day.

There was some difference of opinion as to whether the line was used for passengers during the war. The company claimed that there was never a suspension of the passenger service; only that fewer trains ran during the war. Passenger services were reinstated fully in October 1945. However, only one of the engines, an 0-6-0 saddle tank built by Avonside Engine Company, was working at the time. The Corringham Railway was one of those not included in the nationalisation of the railways after the war.

90. The Blackpool to Manchester Victoria train at Bolton. The town was seriously damaged by bombing during the war.

Supplies for the large number of American troops who would take part in the invasion of Europe were arriving from America at ports in South Wales and Cornwall. These goods were moved by train towards the south coast and would eventually be taken across to France.

The increase in trains in 1943 from the earlier years of the war was quite profound. On the GWR there were roughly 400 troop trains a month early in the year. By November, the number had risen to 1,000. Many of these were to carry American forces from their landing points in Wales and Cornwall to the south coast. After the troops had alighted from the trains the guard and driver would walk through to see what they had left. The Americans were so well supplied that the railway staff often did quite well out of what they had left on the trains.

There was a lucky escape for passengers in Middlesbrough in November when a bomb fell on the station just after a train had left. The bomb landed in front of the engine of an empty train while another bomb struck a refreshments room. Part of the station roof was brought down, landing on the empty train. The train driver, William Buck of Gateshead, survived, but the fireman, D. Crowfield, also of Gateshead, died of his injuries.

91. Middleborough station in August 1942. A German bomber dropped his bombs on the station, seriously damaging the Victorian glass roof and also causing damage to a train in the station. (*Mirrorpix*)

There was a shortage of coal in December; output averaged 3,662,600 tons a week compared with 3,815,100 in November. One of the reasons for the fall was a serious outbreak of influenza, which had at times led to a loss of 120,000 tons a week more than the normal loss for the period due to illness amongst the miners.

Chapter 8

1944

Austerity locomotives were still being produced in 1944, including a 2-10-0 Austerity loco designed by R.A. Riddles, Director of Transportation Equipment at the Ministry of Supply from 1939, and Chief Stores Superintendent at the LMS from 1943. These engines were built by the North British Loco Company, Glasgow. They entered production in 1943 but were first used in 1944; 150 of them were built, numbered 3650 to 3799.

Manufacture of Austerity 2-8-0s had been started in 1943, with Nos. 7150 to 7449 built up to 1944 at North British Locomotive Company. Also, Nos. 7450 to 7509 were built at the Vulcan Foundry up to 1944; Nos. 8510 to 8624 at North British Locomotive Limited through 1944 and into 1945; and Nos. 8625 to 8718 at the Vulcan Foundry in 1944, as were Nos. 9177 to 9312 through 1944 into 1945.

On 20 January, Lord Leathers, the Minister of War Transport, addressed twenty-two representative railway workers at the Charing Cross Hotel, five of whom were women. The workers were treated to lunch to celebrate the completion of sixty-four of the special utility locomotives that the government had ordered the previous year.

Lord Leathers said that the railways would this year be tried as never before and that the workers had a vital part to play in moving the armies of victory. He then called on the railways to help him in the special programme of building 2-8-0 engines that were urgently needed. Southern had undertaken to build 110. Before the war, Southern had only built ten locomotives a year. They had passed the previous year's planned total of sixty by four.

Locomotives weren't the only things that were being sent to France. At Eastleigh railway depot, along with the troops that arrived there by train were large numbers of freight wagons that had travelled across from America in kit form. They were assembled and sent across for the

92. One of the American locomotives that were shipped to Britain during the war. This is shown later, after D-Day, when it had been moved to France.

American Transport Corps to be used on the French railway system. American engines that had been used on the British railway system during the war also arrived at Eastleigh for eventual shipping to France.

The American engines and goods wagons had arrived at Avonmouth, where they were assembled by American men. One of the train drivers at Bristol remembered the trucks being assembled in minutes. The engines were used at Bristol until they were later sent to France. There were to be about 400 American locomotives operating in Britain during the war. Many of these were shipped across to France after D-Day.

The US Army 2-8-0 Austerity locomotives were ordered by the US Army Transportation Corps for use in Western Europe and were built in America. Designed by Major J.W. Marsh of the railway branch of the US Army Corps of Engineers, they were built by the American Locomotive Company, Baldwin Locomotive Company and Lima Locomotive Company. A number of them were in use in Britain before being sent to Europe.

The US Army 0-6-0 T was an Austerity locomotive built for shunting. It was mainly used in Army depots and dock areas and designed and built for the Transportation Corps. They were built by H.K. Porter and

Company, Vulcan Locomotives and Davenport Locomotive Works in America. Many of these were lent to the British War Department.

The US Army 0-4-4-0 Diesel-Electric was built by the Whitcomb Locomotive Company for the US Transportation Corps but they were initially built for use in Britain. The design was later used for larger diesel locomotives, and these were used in Europe.

The American men recruited into the railway section of the US Transportation Corps came to England with experience of large lines strung out across America. They were not used to the tightly packed density of traffic operating in England. They were not even used to the idea of double tracks, which were used only one way on each track. They saw them as two separate lines. The American railwaymen were also used to larger wagons as their freight tended to travel longer distances without being sorted into different areas. Many of their stations didn't have platforms and so people climbed aboard using steps. There is no doubt that many of the American railwaymen expected to find a railway system in England that had not moved on from Victorian times.

The Americans built a number of railway installations of their own in England, mainly in the west, such as at Blinkhorn, near Taunton, and along the west coast. Much of Devon became American territory for a time and many of the local population were forced to move out. The installations were used for the landing of American troops and equipment but some were also built in the east to supply the American airbases.

The American railway resources were eventually moved to Southampton, from where they would reach France. There were 279 locomotives, 674 American freight wagons and 269 other railway vehicles including six ambulance trains of fifteen coaches, and twenty-six cranes. Most of these went across on three train ferries but some locomotives went on landing craft.

The Times started the year with a report that 'Somewhere in England', soldiers of the American and British armies, most of whom were railwaymen in civil life, were engaged in a ceaseless task of assembling railway rolling stock. The stock was destined for use when the invasion of 'Hitler's Fortress' began. It was estimated that 50 miles of new rolling stock would be ready on invasion day. Prefabricated parts had been brought from America, saving by the process of transportation about

93. Horwich Locomotive Works, near Bolton, started life in the late nineteenth century for the Lancashire and Yorkshire Railway. It had its own 18-inch gauge railway within the works. It became part of the LMS in 1923. It had produced shells during the First World War.

94. The Horwich Works played a large part in training well-known names on the railway as three of the Big Four had chief mechanical engineers who did at least part of their apprenticeship there. They were George Hughes and Harry Fowler, LMS, Richard Maunsell, SR, and Nigel Gresley, LNER. During the war, the works produced a number of different tanks for the army.

25 per cent of the shipping space that would have been used if the trucks were sent complete.

Many of the men of the American Army Railway Unit were trained in the United States railway centre at New Orleans and at workshops at Bucyrus Ohio. They were assembling prefabricated boxcars at the rate of one per hour. The cars were being built in an enormous assembly shop with six tracks running through it.

An officer was in charge of each line with a non-commissioned officer in charge of each section. The assembled parts for seven types of cars were passed into marshalling yards from the assembly line every hour. One battalion composed of men from Pennsylvania Railroad Company had been turning out thirty American-sized cars a day. The battalion also operated a transport depot where rolling stock was held in readiness for shipment to Europe.

Included in the vehicles were 40-ton refrigerator cars, 20- and 50-ton gondola cars, 10,000-gallon tank cars, 55-ton flat cars and 20-ton boxcars and brake vans. There were also special troop-carrying cars and hospital units. All the rolling stock was of standard gauge used in America, England and on the Continent. The assembly shop was stocked with American tools and equipment. Several British dining cars had been adapted for use as a hospital train. Tiers of beds were fitted in a number of these coaches. Others contained accommodation for stretchers, a pharmacy and operating theatres.

The officer in command of the unit was Lieutenant Colonel H.U. Bates, a former general shop and engine house foreman for the Pennsylvania Railroad. Major General Frank S. Ross, Chief of Operations of Transportation in the European theatre, had visited the site and said, 'We can erect any kind of rolling stock here that we intend to use.'

* * *

There was some doubt about the extent of fatalities when two trains collided at Ilford on 16 January 1944. *The Times* stated the following day that fifteen had died whereas the LNER had said that only one had died. The actual number was nine. The two trains were both bound for Liverpool Street; the one from Norwich ran into the rear of one from

Yarmouth. Most of the casualties were in the rear coach of the Yarmouth train. It was a strange coincidence that fatal accidents had occurred at Ilford in both world wars.

The injured were treated by civil defence rescue squads and by both British and American servicemen. As well there being some American servicemen on the platform at the time of the collision, there were also many on the train. The routes were often used by Americans travelling from the numerous bases in East Anglia on their way to London.

One of the casualties had not been on the train, according to the *Manchester Guardian* a few days after the accident. An ARP worker had run from his post to help and had run into a wall. He later died from his injuries. Another fatality was Frank Heilgers, former MP for Bury St Edmunds. Others killed included six British people and three Americans; many more Americans were taken to hospital.

The jury at the inquest considered that the accident was due to the inefficient system of detonators between Shenfield and Ilford. A detonator is a small device that explodes when a train runs over it. They were used on the line when it was foggy. The signalman at Seven Kings, Ilford, said that the Norwich train should have stopped at the danger signal before the station. The driver said he did not see it. The coroner told him that if he did not see it he should have treated it as at danger. The signalman had phoned Ilford to try to get the Norwich train stopped. A fog man had arrived at the signal ten minutes after the Norwich train had passed. The signal was also on the side that was normally read by the fireman.

There was a serious disaster at Catterick Bridge station, close to Catterick Garrison, on 4 February, when a railway truck being loaded with shells exploded, killing twelve and injuring up to a hundred. The event showed how important was the training that had been conducted by the army for men involved in working on the wartime railways. It was thought that the explosion may have been due to the incorrect loading of the explosives.

The Times reported the incident on 7 February, but of course did not give the location beyond saying that it was in the north of England. The report described it as an army and RAF ammunition truck loading on a railway siding and that some of the dead were serving army and

RAF personnel. *The Times* gave the number of dead as ten, with seventy injured. The railway station and signal box was badly damaged, along with other buildings close by such as the railway hotel and some houses.

Railway staff were amongst the fatalities: Walter Gibson, the stationmaster, had both legs amputated but later died in hospital. Mrs Mary Richmond and Miss Nancy Richardson, both clerks at the station, also died. Lancelot Rymer and William Tindall, motor drivers, died, as did Luen Jenkins RAF and Lieutenant Lawrence King of the radio telephone operator staff, who was on duty at the station. A witness said that two or three trucks seemed to have been blown to pieces while others were on fire. Buildings around the station were damaged or burning. Passengers waiting on the platform were injured. A bus passing by was also damaged and a taxi had its roof blown off but the driver was uninjured. The taxi driver ran along the line to stop a train that was approaching the site of the explosion.

A War Office statement said that it regretted to announce that during loading ammunition trucks at a northern railway station, an explosion occurred, causing casualties among civilian and service personnel. They gave the figures as six service personnel and four civilians killed. Of the six servicemen, four were army and two were RAF.

The inquest under Lieutenant Colonel John Symons, officer commanding an RAOC unit, stated that a War Office court of inquiry revealed that every precaution had been taken at the railway station and the rules for handling explosives had been followed. The cause of the explosion could not be ascertained. The final death count was twelve.

There is always a feeling that everyone was doing their utmost to facilitate the war effort during the conflict so it is surprising to find that unions were still active in trying to raise wages while men were fighting overseas. In March, three railway unions asked for a flat rate increase of twelve shillings a week. This was a single claim by the NUR, ASLEF and the Railway Clerks' Association (RCA). The fact that it was a single claim was to ensure that there was not the same ill feeling that there had been the previous year when the enginemen had demanded different treatment from other staff. The claim for twelve shillings was the same amount that had previously been awarded to surface workers at collieries, which included men working in colliery railway sidings. There had been

95. Trains carrying weapons were a common sight during the war. This train is carrying Sherman tanks, probably on their way to a port in southern England ready to cross to Normandy. (*Mirrorpix*)

an increase in wages the previous June of four shillings and sixpence a week. That increase had been payable to women as well as men, while the previous increase at the end of 1942 had been five shillings for men and three shillings and ninepence for women.

In the spring, the railway system was busy moving troops towards the south coast, mainly concentrated on Southampton but also to other ports in the south. The previous year, 15 miles of new sidings had been laid in the New Forest near Lockerley. The sidings were full of wagons in the lead-up to D-Day and were hidden by the trees from prying enemy eyes.

Alongside the new sidings were 134 large sheds for supplies for the American troops. The increase in traffic was evident and was shown at the small station at Dunsbridge in the Southern section. In June 1938, 182 wagons had passed through the station, and 5,246 passed through in June 1944. The GWR were just as busy in the six months leading up to D-Day, when they ran 18,609 trains carrying troops and equipment towards the south coast ports.

The number of American troops in Britain had increased in 1944, but their presence wasn't always positive. Some American servicemen were based at a place called Henstridge, near Templecombe, on the Somerset and Dorset Railway. They included the General Service Engineer Group, who were involved in local building work helping to maintain supply lines for D-Day. Some of the bridges in the area were not strong enough for heavy traffic and were being upgraded.

On 13 March, a troop train was ready to move from Bath with a double locomotive and ten carriages. The two engines were needed due to some of the steep gradients on the line to Bournemouth. As the train approached Henstridge station, what was believed to be an American forces lorry that was crossing a bridge above the track went out of control and crashed through the parapet and on to the train below. The front engine broke free and derailed the second engine and some of the following coaches. There were an unconfirmed number of deaths – probably between one and six – but, as with most accidents at the time, there was little publicity around it. Unlike other accidents of the period, there does not seem to have been a published accident investigation report.

A select committee of the government decided in March that there should be a cessation in the call-up of railway workers and that a steady influx of labour should be directed to the railways. In spite of all that had been done to impress upon the public that they should be travelling as little as possible, further efforts were needed in this direction. People were also advised that they should stagger their holiday times.

The report claimed that there was no shortage of railway wagons but a scarcity had been created because of the time it was taking to unload them. Blackout restrictions were partly to blame but a more important factor was the lack of engines and operational staff needed to clear sidings.

The congestion on the railways had also aggravated a serious situation at collieries, where filled wagons were not being moved. In some areas, coal was stockpiled at pitheads, which made miners reluctant to work at maximum effort when the coal they had dug was not carried away. Before further calls were made on the railway it was essential to clear the accumulation of goods and coal that were waiting for transport.

Despite the problems, the report went on to say that the railways were still being denuded of men who were being directed to other industries.

96. While many of the railway-owned workshops were producing armaments for the government, private companies such as the Birmingham Railway Carriage and Wagon Company Limited were producing railway equipment. This is an exhibition poster from 1910, which was still being used as an advert in a wartime magazine.

There were, according to the report, limits as to how much women could be substituted for men, so there was an urgent need for a steady influx of male labour.

There were only sixty-five dining cars left on the railways at this point in the war and they were withdrawn for the Easter holidays. This had been a normal event during wartime but the difference this time was that they would not be coming back after the holidays. The years of war had whittled away the luxuries for the railway passenger and the dining cars had been a reminder of happier times when travelling.

The meeting of the board of the Birmingham Railway Carriage and Wagon Company took place in April. One of the points discussed were the difficulties faced by companies during the war and how they were looking forward to the removal of restrictions once the war ended. The company did survive, however, and went on producing railway vehicles until it closed shortly after the demise of the steam engine.

In May, an announcement by the Railway Executive Committee stated that because of the increasing pressure on the railways, it would need to withdraw without notice many more passenger trains during the summer. The public were advised to avoid travelling, especially long distances. Despite the warning, the railway companies made alternative arrangements for those trains cancelled so that there was minimum inconvenience to the public. An official at Paddington said that they didn't know from one day to the next which trains would run. A spokesman at Euston said that it was in the hands of the authorities. There were no routes closed from Waterloo and Victoria, although there were some cancellations. Trains were cancelled from Liverpool Street and King's Cross, and those that did run were very busy.

Despite the appeal from the Railway Executive Committee, a few days later there were reports in the press of tremendous railway traffic to the Newmarket races. This was raised by Mr E.W. Macmillan at the annual conference of the Civil Service in London. He said that it should be the government who should decide whether travel was in the national interest and it should not be left up to an unofficial body.

There is no doubt that the increased pressure was due to the build-up to D-Day. The date was, of course, not known at that time, but it must have been obvious to anyone who knew anything about the railways that there was an enormous amount of military equipment and numbers of men being moved southwards. Because of this, there were further requests from Parliament to the public not to travel unless it was absolutely necessary. There were fears that inland transport might become bottlenecked when the great assault began. Every sacrifice that the public made would be of direct assistance to the troops who would man the ships and fly the airplanes on the day.

There was an unusual court case heard in May when Mrs Alice Greenfield from Parkeston, Essex, claimed damages for the death of her husband. She maintained that the LNER's negligence had led to his death on 3 March 1943 between Shenfield and Ingatestone because they had failed to maintain a safe system of working.

Mr Greenfield was an engine driver employed on the LNER and had been driving a train past Shenfield. Sometime before this, a bomb had dropped on the line and Mr Greenfield was warned to proceed slowly as it was also dark. On reaching the spot where the bomb had landed, the engine fell into the crater. The driver and the fireman were both killed. Mr Justice Charles gave judgement that there had been shortcomings on the part of the railway, who ought not to have sent the train along the line. However, he sided with the company's claim that the injuries were war injuries caused by the dropping of the bomb. They had said that they were not responsible for damages and that injuries sustained through war were covered by a scheme by which compensation was payable out of public funds.

The increase in numbers of women on the railway did not always correspond with upgraded facilities for them. According to a report in the *Manchester Guardian*, women workers at a large London depot said that they had to go to public washhouses ten minutes away from where they worked. It was either this or carry water up a spiral staircase to the mess room, where it had to be boiled.

The newspaper related that there were 500 women employed in the depot and the Essential Work Order, introduced by Minister of Labour Ernest Bevin in March 1941, stated that satisfactory provision for welfare must be made. Most of these 500 women had access to only five lavatories between them, which had been condemned as unfit for men. Five more had been added but were inconveniently placed. Although there were washbasins, there was no hot water, soap or towels. The mess room was sparsely furnished with a trestle table and wooden benches. When the reporter visited he found that there were five girls trying to wash sharing a single bucket. The women had nowhere to change out of dirty clothes and no lockers. There wasn't a nurse on site and the first aid room was staffed by men.

Transporting dangerous loads by train was always a risky business but when a train carrying American bombs caught fire as it approached Soham station on 2 June, it was obviously a very hazardous situation. The train had left Whitemoor marshalling yard in Cambridgeshire on its way to Ipswich, pulled by a War Department Austerity 2-8-0 engine, No. WD7337, consisting of fifty-one wagons, forty-four of them carrying explosives.

97. A number of the railway workshops suffered bomb damage during the war. This was one of them, although the location isn't named.

The fire was in the first coach, and the driver, Benjamin Gimbert, and fireman, James Nightall, were very brave in unhooking the first coach from the rest of the train and driving it away. As they reached the station they called to the signalman to stop traffic coming in the other direction. The coach exploded while they were speaking to him. The fireman died instantly and the signalman, Frank Bridges, died the next day. Gimbert was badly injured but survived. The guard, Herbert Clarke, was injured but managed to walk to the next signal box to stop any more trains.

The explosion destroyed much of the station as well as a number of houses, and put the town's gasworks out of action. The *Manchester Guardian* reported the next day on how the badly shattered town of Soham was rife with stories of the two brave railway men who drove a blazing wagon of bombs away from the train. Both men were awarded the George Cross. A memorial to the men was unveiled in the town in 2007.

The view that the railways should be nationalised after the war was not a new one and had been put forward at the time of the First World War – an indication that conflict was a spur to discussion on the future running of the railway system. When Major General Gilbert Szlumper, who had been appointed Director General of Supply Services for the Ministry of Supply in 1942, addressed a luncheon of the Engineering Industries Association he went even further in discussing this. He said that it was the duty of industrialists to see that transport in the post-war era was reborn to suit both national and industrial requirements.

Major General Szlumper said that there were three alternatives: transport operations should be returned to pre-war status; transport overall should be administered by private enterprise; or that all transport should be nationalised. He thought that the first option was impossible, the second was desirable, and the third disastrous. The Major General's view was hardly surprising as he had previously been the former general manager of the Southern Railway. His views on nationalisation had been formed by his wartime experience in the War Office, Ministry of Transport, Board of Trade and Ministry of Supply. The more offices he held, the more convinced he had become that the business of government was to govern and not to try to run industries of which they had neither training nor experience. In his view, nationalisation would mean that transport problems would be subordinate to the prevailing political stance since politics permeated all government activities.

98. Many of the locomotives that were sent over from America during the war eventually made their way across to Normandy. Unloading a locomotive could not have been easy on the beaches, as this image shows.

Although the Major General didn't believe in nationalisation, he suggested that all forms of transport, including the railways, should be brought under central control and their revenues and expenditures pooled into a common account. He believed that the efficient use of transport was more important than who actually carried the traffic. This would operate under a National Transport Board.

The Big Four were quick to answer through their chairmen, who seemed to think that the fact that Major General Szlumper was an ex-general manager of the Southern Railway Company meant that they in some way agreed with his ideas. They wished to make it clear that Szlumper was expressing his personal opinion and that they were not views held by the boards of the four mainline companies.

The Labour Party put forward their policy for the railways in June. The executive committee said that transport was a national service that must be unified and co-ordinated under state ownership. There was little doubt that if the Labour Party won the next general election, there was a very good chance the railways would be nationalised. It was a policy that was being implemented in other parts of the world and did not deter voters from electing a post-war Labour government.

The preparations for D-Day and the invasion of Normandy, codenamed Operation Overlord, were perhaps the biggest tests faced by the railway system in the war. Whatever was leaving British ports bound for Europe had to be closely co-ordinated with what was arriving from across the Atlantic. In addition to the railway companies' preparations for the role they were to play in this, the army had been training in the use of railways during the invasion of Europe since the early days of the war. The land-based railway training areas for the army at Longmoor and Melbourne had been added to with the coastal base at Faslane. A further military training port had been set up in 1944 at Cairnryan, on the eastern coast of Loch Ryan, near Stranraer. A new railway line was laid to connect it with the Stranraer lines 6 miles away.

The railwaymen themselves were also involved in the preparations. There had been a meeting of railway workers at Euston earlier in the year, when they had been sworn to secrecy. They had met with Sir Bernard Montgomery, who encouraged them to take part in what was to come. He told them that he was sure he could rely on them to co-operate with the 'utmost possible intensity' in providing transport for the troops.

In the months leading up to June, men, guns, tanks and every other form of military hardware were moved from the hundreds of depots around the country to the concentration areas in the south. The most important aspect of the movement was secrecy. This was mainly the responsibility of the railway system, which moved the bulk of the freight that was involved. The main marshalling areas all lay within easy reach of the embarkation points and stretched along the coast from Cornwall to the Thames. All the southern ports were put into action. Even small coastal villages saw soldiers departing for Normandy.

Once the men and stores arrived in the south, they became the responsibility of the dock workers who had to load them on to the ships that would take them on the final leg of their journey across to the beaches of Normandy. The railways had not quite completed their task, however, as a number of locomotives were loaded on to the ships to accompany the men into Europe.

In the weeks after D-Day, a call went out for volunteer shunters for the docks at Southampton. There was a constant flow of trains going both ways. Supplies were being sent on to ships to cross to France. On their return journeys, the ships were carrying many of the men who had been involved in the D-Day landings who were now coming back for a rest.

The movement of men and equipment towards the south coast continued after D-Day as the men in Europe still had to be supplied. There was also, however, a large amount of movement in the opposite direction, with hospital trains carrying the wounded back from the south. Many of these were American servicemen. Those who were to be repatriated to America were taken to Liverpool or Glasgow.

There were three hospital trains on constant standby: two American and one British. When ships carrying wounded arrived from France, the hospital trains would be moved to the town quay to load the wounded. Also coming back on the ships were large numbers of German prisoners of war. There was a temporary camp with huts surrounded by barbed wire that had been used by Allied troops before D-Day. The prisoners would then be loaded aboard trains and taken to Kempton Park or Newbury Race Course, which had been turned into POW camps. The prisoners were guarded by British troops. If the train had to stop to take on water, the guards would jump out and watch the doors on both sides of the train.

99. Prisoners of war often travelled on the railways under guard, as this military railway voucher shows.

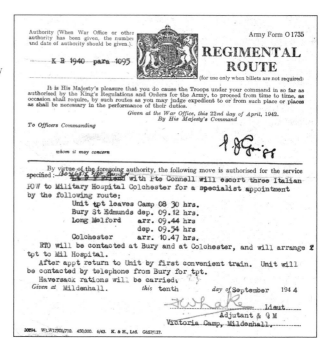

Those on their way to hospital were often taken to Kidderminster for the American hospital near Camp Bewdley, at Wolverley. Twenty hospital trains arrived at Kidderminster in 1944. The camp had been there before the war and was once visited by General Patton. The wounded men were unloaded in the sidings at Kidderminster under armed guard. Locals knew when a train was on its way as all the points were clamped to allow access.

The trains that brought the Americans were Overseas Ambulance Trains, which were pulled by a LNER locomotive class b.12/3. The trains had a permanent crew of two drivers, two firemen, two guards and a fitter. The trains were supposed to be used by the Americans on the Continent.

Although the hospital trains were pulled by LNER locomotives, the Americans had also brought their own locomotives with them as they began to build up their supplies for D-Day. Most of the American engines had been used to pull goods trains. They were painted grey and either had Transportation Corps USA or just USA painted on them. Although many of them had gone to France, some American engines remained in England.

The number of special trains and the items that the invasion force needed was unimaginable. One example was when the invasion force advanced into Holland and the War Office asked for a special train in a hurry for a priority consignment – rubber boots. Seventeen wagons were loaded at Stirling. The train only stopped at Leeds to pick up another fifteen wagons before reaching the south, and the boots were then loaded aboard a steamer for Antwerp.

There was a strange request from Mr Ellis Smith MP when addressing a Trades Council conference of the Lancashire and Cheshire areas in July. It was strange in that so much development work on the railways had been put on hold during the war and when the government were trying to get the public not to travel, and there was little chance of what he was asking for happening. Mr Ellis Smith wanted an increase in the electric railway system to get workers to the seaside and countryside at weekends. He claimed that it would reduce road accidents and the amount of coal being used, which he said was too valuable to be wasted. He wanted an outer circuit electric railway within a 50-mile radius of Manchester, covering Preston, Liverpool, Sheffield, Southport and Morecambe, with an inner circuit of the kind operating in London. Surely the resources needed to build such a system would have been far more costly than the coal that was saved and would add little to the war effort if it was mainly for pleasure.

Whatever the result of the argument about control of the railways after the war would be, there were private companies willing to serve whoever the new masters were. The British Wagon Company in Rotherham claimed to have been supplying railway wagons for more than seventy years. They were at this time advertising in *The Times*, explaining how they sold railway wagons on hire purchase and could also supply all kinds of industrial plant. The advertisement also mentioned how the company had 'remained in the forefront helping industry to respond to the demands of war', while being ready to take part in the task of reconstruction ahead.

The chairman of the company, Mr W.H. Copley, said during a meeting that despite the difficulties during the war, they were still making a profit, although profits had dropped due to the requisitioning of wagons by the government and other restrictions. He went on to say that, while continuing their aid to the war effort, the company was taking all possible steps to ensure that they would be in a position to take advantage of the demand during post-war reconstruction. Mr Copley tendered his good wishes to the seventy-six members of staff who were in the forces. He then informed the meeting of the sad news that three members of the staff serving in the RAF had been reported missing after operations over Germany.

There were a number of meetings going on in 1944, and the annual general meeting of the GWR also took place at the Great Western Royal Hotel, Paddington. The first item on the agenda was to inform the meeting that the chairman of the GWR, Sir Charles Hambro, had been appointed by the Minister of War Transport as the United Kingdom member of the combined raw materials board and head of the British Raw Materials Mission in Washington.

Whilst the net revenue of the company came from the fixed annual payment under the Railway Control Agreement, there was a further payment of £269,379 net income from sources outside the control of the agreement, so it was apparent that the railways did still have other income during the war. There was also a report that a credit of £937,825 arose in relation to 5,000 20-ton wagons that the company had bought ten years before and had let out on redemption hire terms to colliery companies. The agreement had terminated the previous year and the wagons had passed into the ownership of the companies concerned.

The restrictions on renewing vehicles and maintenance on tracks meant that the company was in arrears by about fifteen months on renewal work on maintenance, two years behind on the locomotive building programme and three years behind on passenger train building. The only work the company was permitted to carry out was that which was essential to the war effort.

It seemed as if the dangers of bombing and invasion were decreasing by 1944, although the first few months of the year had seen some increase in attacks on London. The railways were concentrating on moving goods and men to the south coast to keep the invasion force supplied once they had landed. There had been little of the expected air attacks during Operation Overlord. The reason for this became clearer shortly after D-Day.

For some time, there had been rumours of secret weapons in the hands of the Germans. Then a new threat appeared: the V-1 flying bombs, or doodlebugs. Many of the evacuees from previous years had gone home but once the doodlebugs began to fall there was a rapid unofficial attempt by civilians to flee London. Stations were crowded with people, who were often taking with them all they could carry. The government decided on an official evacuation in July, and on 11 July, twenty special trains took 12,550 evacuees away from London.

The arrival of the V-1s was to have another effect on the rail system. It wasn't that the rockets were particularly aimed at the railways; they could have fallen anywhere. However, it seemed that by just bad luck, they caused severe disruption to the system. The new bombs also caused an increase in work for the rail system as anti-aircraft guns and balloons were moved towards the coast as protection from the new weapon.

From 13 June to 31 August, 8,000 flying bombs landed on the country. Forty-two of these damaged railway lines. Hungerford Bridge was hit on 19 June. The centre of Cow Lane Bridge, near Peckham Rye, was destroyed on 13 July; the remains had to be blown up by the Royal Engineers. The stationmaster's house at Folkestone was also destroyed, but this was by shells from France.

The V-1s continued to land across the country for the rest of 1944. Although the rockets could not be aimed at specific targets, many of them fell in the south, in the area around London and on the city itself. The fact that they did some quite serious damage to the railways was just bad luck. It was the Southern Railway area that suffered the most damage from the V-1s.

A number of servicemen from the army and the RAF had been loaned to the railways for the three months coming up to July. They had been trained and were beginning to work as firemen and in engine sheds. They were to receive service pay while employed on the railways. The invasion of France had added to the requirements of railway transport and the most serious shortage of manpower was amongst locomotive staff. The four weeks after D-Day had been the busiest ever for the railways. During the period, there were 17,500 troop and stores trains carrying reinforcements and supplies for the men in France. This was an increase of 33 per cent on the month before D-Day, when 13,000 trains ran. There were a further 113 military mail trains and 300 journeys by ambulance trains.

There were also a large number of special trains to carry German prisoners of war who were brought to the United Kingdom from Europe. The trains carried them from their port of arrival to camps all over the country. During the fourth week after D-Day, there were also 175 special trains from London carrying evacuees as a result of the flying bomb attacks.

The figures for train accidents in the previous year were released in August. There had only been one accident with fatalities, and only four deaths. This was the lowest total for seven years, despite an increase of 20 per cent in traffic. There had been 393 train accidents of all kinds, of which 195 were caused by human failure. There were thirty-four fatalities among passengers and railway staff due to things other than train crashes. This meant that one passenger in 440 million died. The blackout was still a significant factor as of the 145 passenger fatalities in movement accidents, seventy occurred after dark. The introduction of better lighting in the last months of the previous year had undoubtedly improved the situation.

One of the last days of shelling to occur at Dover was on 13 September. Priory Street station was hit and several people were killed. Mr Cooney, the under station manager at Priory Street, kept a diary of the war years. A typical entry was, 'Air raids and all day long bombardment from the French coast'.

One person at the station missed most of the action. The new station manager, Mr Watkins, arrived in September and was just in time for the Germans' last throw before the Allied troops took over the shelling sites. He described it as a final bombardment using all that the Germans had.

Manchester Exchange station had suffered badly from the effects of bombing during the war but its reconstruction led to a bonus for railway staff. Mr H.A. Bailey, the district passenger manager of the LMS, opened a new staff canteen at the station. The canteen replaced one that had been situated in two railway carriages. Mr Bailey said that the reconstruction of the station had taken into account the needs of the staff and the public.

There was obviously still a great deal of interest in the railways during wartime and the use of American locomotives and the Austerity vehicles must have given train spotters a lot to look out for. The success of the co-operation between the American and British railways in the war was commended by Colonel Norman Ryan, Assistant Chief of Transportation US Army. He was speaking while opening a British – US Railway photographic exhibition at the Grosvenor Hotel, Victoria station, in September. The exhibition was dedicated to the men and women of the two nations who, in peace and war, upheld the traditions of railway service. It had been prepared by the Big Four companies along with the United States Army Transportation Corps. The photographs were of both peacetime and wartime railway activities on the British and American railway systems. The exhibition was to tour the country.

The smooth running of the railways sustained a slight problem in September, when 500 LNER drivers and firemen went on strike in Sheffield. The strike was because three of the men's colleagues were summoned for failing to perform fire-watching duties. The strike caused some disorganisation of goods traffic but did not disrupt passenger services.

The magistrates' court was crowded with railwaymen. Mr O.C. Somerville-Jones prosecuting said that the unions' threat that there would be a strike if the men were summoned was a form of blackmail. The Ministry of War Transport would not tolerate this. The three men were fined a pound each but an application for costs was disallowed. The men then returned to work.

Meanwhile in London, the V-1 flying bombs were causing some of the worst destruction on the railways that had occurred since the early days of the conflict. A number of lines were knocked out throughout London, although the damage did not stop the trains running for long. The track and supporting structures were struck near Ravenscourt Park, which led to damage at the viaduct carrying the Piccadilly and the District lines between Hammersmith and Ravenscourt Park. The track was usable again by the next morning.

Another flying bomb fell in almost the same spot a few days later, but again, damage was quickly repaired. Aldersgate station was also damaged and the tunnel roof was pierced, but traffic was only held up for six hours. Passenger agent T. Walker had been buried under debris at Aldersgate but dug himself out to save record books. Another tunnel was damaged between South Kensington and Gloucester Road on the Metropolitan Line. Debris blocked the tracks and gas escaped into the District Line tunnel, stopping the District and Circle lines for thirteen hours.

A flying bomb was close to hitting a train full of passengers at Wimbledon. The driver heard the bomb approaching and stopped the train, and the bomb fell on to the railway bank in front of them. It was only the driver, H. Humphreys, who saved the passengers from harm. At West Ham, 108 trolley buses were damaged and an overhead junction was destroyed.

One of the fastest repairs was achieved by LNER engineers after a bridge was badly damaged between Liverpool Street and Stratford, which carried four tracks. The northern half of the bridge was destroyed and the southern half was broken. Steel joists were fitted on to the bridge and trains were running over it again the next day.

By October, 250 large stations and a number of smaller ones had their lighting improved. There had been 28,000 shades removed and 57,000 more powerful light bulbs fitted on the GWR. On the LMS, work had begun on removing shades from corridor vehicles, involving approximately 100,000 shades, and also on non-corridor vehicles. The LNER was also working on removing shades. The blackout had little effect on the V-1 flying bombs and also the V-2 rockets being fired at the country.

There was an unexpected increase in passengers from Europe towards the end of the year. These were not wounded servicemen but more prisoners of war. It was a well-known fact that British and Allied POWs were not always treated well by the enemy. When they were moved from one place to another, they often travelled in very crowded cattle trucks.

When Josef Kox was captured in Holland in November, he thought he would be treated well by the British but did not expect his experience to be one of comfort. He arrived at Tilbury by ship and then travelled to Fenchurch Street by train. Unlike the British POWs, however, he was surprised to find that he, along with the other German POWs, were carried on a normal passenger train with seats for all of them. Josef was taken to Waterloo by truck and then by another passenger train to Kempton Park.

The war seemed to have gone some way towards ending the class system on British railways, at least until peace was restored. Second class travel had been ended some time before the war, leaving only first or third class. There was some debate over the continuation of first class, not least in letters to *The Times*. There was little doubt that many passengers with third class tickets were using first class carriages due to overcrowding in third class. One first class passenger informed *The Times* that she had seen third class passengers whose tickets had been punched by a railway inspector receiving no comment on their being in the wrong carriage. According to her, the invasion of first class by third class passengers was likely to continue when encouraged by railway officials.

There were a number of letters from first class travellers bemoaning the decline in the standard of travel for those paying for first class who thought encroachment should be stopped. Others felt that the sale of first class tickets may as well be discontinued. There was obviously a great difficulty in not getting into a first class carriage when the door to the carriage stopped

100. There was some argument during the war about passengers with third class tickets travelling in first class carriages when trains were full. The image shows a Southern Railway third class carriage.

in front of passengers while they were standing on a crowded platform. The choice was often, get in first class or not get on the train.

There was a different version of events regarding first class put forward by Inspector Matthews of the LMS police at Salford. He said that special examiners were being put on trains as nobody was allowed to travel in a first class carriage with a third class ticket whatever the circumstances. This was at the trial in October of Dennis Warne of Higher Broughton, who was charged with travelling in a first class carriage on a workman's ticket despite being told to leave by the train guard. Warne claimed that the newspapers said that third class ticket holders were permitted to travel in a first class compartment if there were no third class seats available. Mr R. Almack, prosecuting for the railway, claimed that what was taking place was a rush for the first class compartments when a train arrived. It was only once the first class carriages were full that passengers went to third class. Warne denied this, claiming that there were no third class seats available and that workers had to stand on trains night after night while first class carriages were empty. Warne had asked his union, the Amalgamated Engineers, to take his case.

There had been some dispute throughout the wartime period about the amount that the government were paying the railways. Mr P.J. Noel Baker, parliamentary secretary to the Minister of War, denied in the House of Commons that the railway companies had a raw deal from the government. He said that the government had to make the best bargain from the taxpayers' point of view and one that was also acceptable to the railway chairmen.

The question had been raised by Sir John Mellor, MP for Tamworth, who said that the terms had been forced by political pressure down the throats of the railway companies, who had swallowed them in fear of worse deals being forced upon them.

There was a renewed protest by the Railway Stockholders' Union in December complaining that the rental agreement between the government and the railway companies had never been put before the owners. The complaints were said to be proof that problems remained to be settled in relation to control of the railways after the war ended.

There was also dispute over the question of wear and tear of railway stock during the war years. Under the agreement, the railway companies could only claim for repairs and renewals at the same rate as applied in the years 1935–37. There had, however, been abnormal wear due to the high pressure exerted on the railways during the war.

Lord Royden, chairman of the LMS, stated that very large sums had had to be spent on repairs to locomotives and rolling stock, and these were not provided for in the trust fund. The trust fund was to make good repairs after the war but it had been used to make repairs during the war to keep the railways running. At the end of the First World War, the government had admitted liability for making good abnormal wear and tear.

The attempts by the government to dissuade the public from travelling during the war had never been a success. As Christmas approached, railway staff in the Manchester area were likely to have to deal with the heaviest Christmas demand since 1939. The morning trains for London and the south were densely packed with passengers who were not on business as it was evident from the luggage they carried that they were taking a holiday.

At Exchange station, there had been heavy bookings for North Wales, and from Manchester Victoria, every train leaving for Blackpool and other parts of the Lancashire coast were crowded. Railway officials were expecting a harassing festive season as Christmas Day was on a Monday, meaning the holiday would be longer than normal. The existing services available barely coped with normal levels of customers and if people wanted to travel, they would have to put up with discomfort.

It wasn't only the public who were trying to use the railways to get away for Christmas. There had been an escape of ninety-seven Italian prisoners from a camp in Ayrshire. On 21 December, an Italian paratrooper officer and a sergeant major were found in the Ayrshire village of Dalrymple in a railway wagon standing in some sidings. The driver of a passing train had seen the men and recognised their prison uniforms.

There was a feeling of making good six years of forced neglect of the railways as the year drew to an end. One of the first items on the programme was to clean and repaint rolling stock, stations and equipment. According to *The Times*, the whole country was in need of a through spring cleaning. They looked forward to the return of faster trains, sleeping and restaurant cars, and new coaches. All of these had been promised, but the end of 1944 was a bit too soon as the war still had to be won and the programme of renewal would not begin until the war ended.

Chapter 9

1945

The railways had a group of celebrity passengers in early January and they put on a reserved coach for them on the 8.45 Euston to London Road, Manchester. They were twenty-five men from a troopship carrying the first men on leave who had taken part in the invasion of Europe. There had been men from other parts of the country on the ship, but these were Manchester men.

More men on leave from Europe arrived a few days later and two special trains were run from the port where they had arrived to the north of England and Scotland. The LNER claimed that the trains were the finest expresses drawn by the powerful Royal engines *Springbok* and *Gazelle*. There was no third class and the trains had chromium-plated and leather-upholstered buffet cars. The LMS took over the trains at Stafford.

Most of the men had been unable to inform their families that they were coming home. Private J. Chesworth of Rawtenstall said that the first thing he was going to do was have a pint. Some of the men were eager to show off souvenirs, such as Private W. Ashworth of Hollingwood, who had a swastika flag and an SS skull and crossbones ring. They were welcomed by canteen workers giving them hot drinks and were offered beds at King George's Club while officers were offered accommodation at the YMCA at Peter Street. The accommodation was not needed as the men wanted only to get home as soon as possible.

There was a report on Southampton in *The Times* on 6 January praising the work carried out by the people of Southampton, saying that the town had suffered heavily in the Blitz, with much of its peacetime work transferred elsewhere. The approach of D-Day had led to extension work on the Southern Railway when new sidings and a signal box were built, and American shunting engines arrived. Secret work had been going on in the city's George V dock. It was where the prefabricated harbour used at Arromanches was made. It led local people to believe that things were improving at a time when they were not certain what was going on.

The biggest sign of progress in the wartime railways had been the 'Woolworths depot'. It was so called because it supplied everything for use overseas, from nuts and bolts to a tank engine. The depot was situated at Micheldever station in Hampshire. The terminus included seventeen marshalling sidings and a 2,000-foot shed, which operated twenty-four hours a day with up to 1,000 wagons arriving every day.

There was a change in the weather towards the end of January when blizzards spread across Scotland and northern England. LNER and LMS officials had a fight to keep trains running and were using sixty snow ploughs along the east coast. Beyond Aberdeen, 350 soldiers were put at the disposal of the LNER to help clear tracks. At Hart, near Hartlepool, 60 yards of the platform was blown on to the tracks.

In early February, Private Edwin James Spence, a Canadian soldier, was killed at Esher when a Waterloo to Portsmouth motor train ran into the rear of a Bournemouth steam train. The driver of the motor train said that he thought a red light was a signal, but it was the light on the back

101. Railway workshops must have been noisy places with a lot of heavy work taking place. This image shows a throat plate being pressed at Swindon.

of the steam train. The driver had applied the brakes and lay down on the floor. He was told by the coroner that he had saved more lives. Albert King, the signalman at Esher West, said he could not account for the accident as he had only cleared one train on the down line.

Although the war was still being fought in Europe there were signs that plans were being made for the post-war position of the railways. At the meeting of the Westinghouse Brake and Signal Company in late February, it was reported that during the war they had experienced a shortage of labour, in common with other railway manufacturers. To combat this, the company had organised outworking depots in small villages, where the women had become their workers. It was an ideal situation as the villages had been in remote areas where transport to factories would have been quite difficult for workers.

The business at the meeting went on to discuss how orders for the company products were increasing and that the shortages endured in the war years would lead to a build-up in demand for replacements and new orders. The company was said to be in a position to expand and fulfil its orders.

A great quantity of explosives and military supplies were still being carried on the railway system in March, and at Bootle, Cumbria, there was a fatal accident involving munitions. Engine driver Harold Goodall, of Workington, had worked for the LMS for thirty-one years. While he was driving a freight train, one of the wagons carrying depth charges caught fire and was noticed by a signalman. Goodall stopped the train and uncoupled the wagon before driving the rest of the train to safety. After sending the fireman down the line to warn other trains of the danger, Goodall went back to see what he could do about the wagon. It then exploded, killing him and leaving a 50-foot deep crater. The explosion was heard 50 miles away.

The V-2 rockets continued to fall on the country into 1945, and again, a lot of damage was done to the railway system. While the Southern had suffered most from the V-1s, it was the LNER that suffered worst from the V-2s. Much damage was caused on the LNER lines connecting London with Essex, Hertfordshire and Middlesex.

One of the most serious V-2 attacks took place on 8 March, when a rocket fell on Smithfield Market. The rocket penetrated into the railway tunnels underneath the market, which contained the market sidings. Many of the buildings fell into the hole made by the blast. The market had been very busy and 110 people died, many of whom were women and children.

Despite the continuing bombing raids, the chairmen of both the LMS and the LNER were asking the government about the future of railway charges. They stated that the highly profitable basis on which the railway had been operating since the Railway Control Agreement of 1941 was due to wartime influences.

There were already indications that government control of the railways would continue for two years instead of the minimum one year originally agreed. There was a view that the rise in the price of coal would be permanent, as would higher wages. Both chairmen estimated that the cost of peacetime travel levels may increase by up to 50 per cent, while there had only been a 16 per cent rise in freight charges.

The chairman of the GWR also had something to say about the post-war railway system. Sir Charles Hambro, at their annual meeting at Paddington in March, said that in his view, the mainline rail companies should continue as four separate entities. Co-ordination on all forms of internal transport should be effected in a way to secure users a free choice of alternative facilities. The GWR were contemplating a large programme of construction of new locomotives and carriages over the next five years. Sir Charles added that he hoped for an improvement in the post-war earnings and that based on the pre-war levels of traffic, charges would have to be raised by about 50 per cent.

102. A blue plaque at Stockport station commemorating the arrival of evacuees from the Channel Islands. (*Gillian Mawson*)

Meanwhile, as the chairmen of the railway companies were putting forward their views on post-war transport, so was Sir Cyril Hurcomb, Director General of the Ministry of War

Transport. He said that an ideally co-ordinated system of transport was one that was best suited in relation to public demand. Cost was far from the only factor and it remained to be seen whether the problem of charges should be dealt with separately, in advance of other features of the future situation.

Sir Cyril went on to say that 'surely the war had taught us something?' and that the four mainline companies would have operated as a unified system for seven years at least. He thought that the habit of co-operation in times of stress added to the knowledge and experience gained and would be found to have contributed much. He went on to say that no one disputed the need for co-ordination of all forms of transport conducted under the baton of a minister. There seemed to be a strong hint there that the return to four separate companies was not seen as the best thing for the country.

With the surrender of Germany in May, there was no further danger to the public or the railways in Britain. Although the war in the Far East was still being fought, it was too far away to affect those at home. It was, however, the time for there to be consideration of what would happen to the railways now that the conflict had ended.

On the south coast of England, the towns closest to the French Coast had had to deal with long-range shelling as well as air raids. In Dover, the town's population had fallen from 40,000 to 23,000, and many of those remaining had been living in caves. After D-Day and the clearing of the French coast, the shelling came to an end. The station foreman at Priory station, who had been there through it all, commented about the end of the shelling, saying, 'I felt blooming queer.'

The danger had not ended for everyone and on the colliery railway of the Wigan Coal Corporation, near Wigan Junction, an unusual event occurred. Ludovic Berry, a locomotive driver, was shunting a train of thirteen wagons loaded with coal. The engine was at the rear of the train. The first wagon suddenly disappeared into a large hole. This was followed by the other twelve, and then the engine. The brakeman at the front of the train had rushed back to warn the driver, but it was too late and he fell into the hole with his engine. The earth around the hole was breaking away, making rescue impossible. Berry had been a driver for the colliery since 1908.

The end of the war led to the release of some but not all secrets. It was revealed in the *Manchester Guardian* that the summit of Mount Snowdon had played a covert part in the war effort, although what this was hadn't been revealed. However, the hotel at the top of the mountain had been reopened and the mountain railway, closed to the public in 1941, was also reopened.

There was obviously a great deal of secrecy during the war to prevent information getting back to the enemy. When British Railways Press Office published *It Can Now be Revealed: More about British Railways in Peace and War* in 1945, this was one of the points they raised. It was mentioned how the goodwill of the public was paramount in railway prosperity and this was not easy to maintain when the public could not be taken into their confidence as it was in peacetime. The book was a detailed explanation of how the railways had been responsible for producing armaments as well as repairing their own materials, how troops were moved to where they were needed and, essentially, how the railways had played their part in the final victory while still providing a decent service to the public. So much of the success of the railways in the war was due to their workshops.

By 1945, the Southern area had four main railway works: at Eastleigh, Brighton, Lancing and Ashford. The works had become more specialised after the amalgamation of the Big Four. Eastleigh was mainly concerned with locomotives, Ashford with freight trucks, Lancing with carriages, and Brighton, which had nearly closed in 1925, with locomotives. The Brighton works had employed 253 men in 1939, but by 1943, it employed 755 men, 218 full-time and thirty-eight part-time women. As well as building locomotives during the war for the Southern, it also supplied them for other rail companies and the military, in addition to making parts for tanks and anti-aircraft guns.

Ashford had been a railway town for many years. The Newtown area was built by the railway for its staff. As well as making trucks for home use, it had also made flat-pack trucks for Russia, which were put together after being delivered to the Persian Gulf and then sent on to Russia. The first trucks were made from pine but as this ran short, oak was used. Part of the works became known as the Joe Stalin Shop.

As well as making locomotives, the Eastleigh works also produced barrels for guns, landing craft, aircraft parts, barges and tanks. Alongside making carriages, the Lancing works had also converted restaurant cars to hospital carriages.

Many of the jobs at the Southern works were done by women. Although women had worked for the railways before the war, they had been mainly employed in clerical jobs. During the war, they also took on the roles of blacksmith, crane driver, electrician and welder.

On the GWR, the Swindon works – possibly being the largest railway works in the world – had to provide shelters for 12,000, and staff had to work as ARP wardens or fire-watchers when not on duty. The glass roof at the works had been painted black. There was a 5-acre timber yard and all that the fire-watchers had to combat any fires were buckets and stirrup pumps. Staff were expected to work very long hours, and this led to some anomalies. Young women who were employed there in their various roles often came from railway families. Due to their long working hours, they often earned more money than their fathers who were employed on the railway rather than in the works. Many of them kept their earnings secret to avoid arguments. Because they worked such long hours, they often had no time to spend what they earned.

Government proposals for bringing the country's inland transport services under public ownership were made known on 28 November 1946, when the text of the Transport Bill was published. The bill proposed to establish a British Transport Commission with the resources to carry goods and passengers by road, rail and inland waterways, and to provide port facilities. It was proposed to bring the Big Four and fifty-six other railway undertakings, with over 52,000 miles of track and 585,152 privately owned wagons, under public ownership. There were to be five bodies appointed; those concerned with the railway system were the Railway Executive and the London Passenger Transport Executive.

Compensation for the railways was to be based on market values on certain dates and would be paid in British Transport stock issued by the commission of a value equal, in the opinion of the Treasury, of that on the date of issue. There were a number of light railways and small railways that were not to be included in the nationalisation scheme. Some of these were dock and colliery railways.

Chapter 10

Reflection

At the end of the war, Winston Churchill said, 'London is like some huge prehistoric animal capable of enduring terrible injuries, mangled and bleeding from many wounds and yet preserving its life and movement.' What kept the animal moving was its transport system and in no uncertain terms that was mainly due to the railway system in the city.

The metaphor should not only apply to London, however. It could be said to relate to the whole country: it was the railway system that managed to keep *that* animal alive and moving as well. Much of the publicity relating to those who fought the war goes to the military. The men and women who ran the railway transport system during the conflict did, in many cases, as much to put their lives on the line for the country as did the military.

There seems to have been a clear separation between the members of the forces and the public during the war with a sort of semi-military middle ground that included the Home Guard, ARP wardens and the fire services. Reading about the actions of railway staff while writing this book has made me think that perhaps they were closer to the semi-military middle ground than they were to members of the public. This, of course, included women as well as men.

This was especially true in the cities, where the railway system – the lifeline of the country – was a prime target for the enemy trying to disrupt the transport system. The smaller towns and country locations did not escape unscathed. Wherever the enemy struck, they were thwarted by men and women prepared to go beyond their normal duties to keep the railway system moving.

The introduction of women into the railway workforce was by no means a universally popular move. It is simple enough to find very opposed opinions. Some managers who labelled women as less conscientious than men may have been unlucky in the women that were sent to them. Those who thought that women were better workers may have been influenced by pretty young women. There was obviously good and bad on both sides of the fence, but there is little doubt that the introduction of women eased the situation in an industry starved of workers. Evan John, in his book *Timetable for Victory*, related that he had spoken to a number of railwaymen who were of the opinion that women railway workers were less likely to show much initiative and preferred routine work. They also complained less at its monotony. This would possibly reflect the fact that women of the era were not generally used to working outside the home or in domestic service, and generally had little experience of factories and less confidence in dealing with workplace situations.

When they were first called upon to supplement the workforce in the railways, there was a belief that it would take three women to replace two men. This did not turn out to be the case, but then, surely, the experience of women having worked in industry and transport during the First World War was evidence enough that they could hold their own in the workplace, and any negative opinions were based on sexist views.

It was also very clear that just as the running of the railways by the government in the First World War opened debates as to how they should be run when the hostilities ceased, the same issues were raised again during the Second World War. There were obviously many conflicting views about what should happen at the end of the war but this time, nationalisation did come about when the Labour government took office. Nationalisation had always been their policy, but they had not been in a position to implement it until they came to power.

Some of the most poignant images of the wartime railways are those of trains full of armaments or men being pulled by steam engines. Nowadays, steam engines invoke a more nostalgic recollection of the era than diesel or electric engines, but this is in hindsight. Those who were trying to keep the railways running, when a steam locomotive consisted of up to 3,000 parts, any one of which could break at any time, leading to a lot of hard, dirty work, would perhaps not look back so fondly.

Whatever the difficulties involved, the romantic appeal of the steam engine endures, as is evidenced by the resurrection of so many heritage railway lines and the restoration of their historic rolling stock. Thankfully, there was a strong workforce consisting of both men and women who were up to the task of keeping them running, which was why British railways did so much to help win the war.

It is strange, then, that the railways, once seen as so vital in difficult times that they needed to be under government control, were so easily discarded back into private hands in the recent past – a move that has not always been successful. The reintroduction of some historic names – such as Great Western and the London and North Eastern – for modern train companies does little to hide that fact. Hopefully, there will never be a time when there is such a serious situation that the railways need to be taken back under government control.

Afterword

Heritage Railways

I had always viewed the value of heritage railways as being a way of keeping steam locomotion alive after it had been abandoned by British Railways. The reality is that many of the heritage railways also have some diesel locomotives. It is also a fact that the concept of the heritage railways movement came about much earlier than I had assumed – well before the last days of steam.

When Sir Henry Haydn Jones – the man responsible for keeping the Talyllyn Railway in operation – died, there was a meeting at the Imperial Hotel in Birmingham. Jones had owned a slate quarry and the railway had originally been used to carry the slate. It was later to become the first narrow gauge railway using steam haulage to carry passengers after an Act of Parliament allowed it. When the railways were nationalised after the war, the Talyllyn Railway was not one of those included in the nationalisation. The meeting took place in 1950, when steam was still at its height on Britain's nationalised railways. The meeting of interested men had the idea of forming a voluntary society to run what was still a public railway. In 1951, it became the first heritage railway run by volunteers in the world.

The days of steam trains, which did so much to win the war for Britain, may be long past. However, it is still possible to experience the type of engines and trains that were common then on Britain's heritage railways. There are over a hundred narrow and standard gauge railways in England alone. Although many of these were branch lines closed by Dr Beeching in the 1960s, most have important wartime connections.

The Colne Valley Railway in Essex had a busy war. As early as September 1939, the railway was carrying thousands of emergency rations to the area for the large number of evacuees expected to arrive at Halstead. As well as having transported these children, it later carried

103. Hythe station on the Romney, Hythe and Dymchurch Railway. The line was taken over by the military in the Second World War and a small armoured train ran on the line, which has a 15-inch gauge.

many airmen. Essex had twenty-seven wartime airfields, and the village of Earls Colne was the location of an American base until 1944. Later arrivals at Halstead were German and Italian POWs who were held at the camp near the town.

The Colne Valley Railway has since preserved its wartime history. The line was closed to passengers in 1962 and freight in 1965. In 1974, a preservation society was formed but the line no longer had any track. Since then, it has gone from strength to strength. Many of the locomotives now used on the line date back to the pre-war era and, no doubt, also played their part in the conflict. Some have notable wartime connections, such as the Hunslet Austerity 0-6-0 locomotives WD190 and WD200, built for the War Department, and the *Blue Star*, No. 35010 Merchant Navy class, built in 1942.

The Hunslet Austerity locomotives are quite common on heritage railways. Peak Rail also has one. Unlike some heritage railways that were individual lines, the Peak Rail line was part of the Midland Railway route from Manchester to London. This therefore played a very important part in the war, as all the lines to London from the north of the country did.

Peak Rail also has a Robert Stephenson and Hawthorns' War Department locomotive built in 1944, and a Drewry/Vulcan Foundry loco, built in 1945.

Many of the heritage railways make a huge effort to remember the war years. An ex-LMS Stanier class 8F loco, No. 8233, had been built as WD307 in 1940. After use on the LMS, it was taken back by the War Department and used by the Royal Engineers to supply Russia. It returned to the UK in 1952 and was used at Longmoor until 1957. After use on British Railways, it eventually ended up on the Severn Valley Railway. On 27 September 1986, at Highley, Shropshire, the locomotive was dedicated as the official memorial to all British military railwaymen who gave their lives on active service in the Second World War, when plaques commemorating the locomotive's service in Persia and Egypt were unveiled.

Many of the heritage railways promote a wartime atmosphere as well as maintaining the locomotives and rolling stock of the era. The Dart Valley Railway, for instance, has an authentic feel of the old GWR, and at Buckfastleigh station, the old GWR benches and chocolate and cream paint hark back to the height of the GWR's heyday and the important part the company played in the war. The railway also has a United States Army Transportation Corps 2-8-0 WD Austerity locomotive.

The Dart Valley Railway became a heritage railway in 1969, and in 1972 took over Dartmouth Steam Railway. It is now called the South Devon Railway. The Dartmouth area was an important shipbuilding site during the war and was also the base of Free French units. The location was heavily bombed during the conflict and the railway was an important supply route.

Although not all heritage railways have Second World War stock, many have important wartime connections. There were some old railway lines that were never very busy until the war began, and that was when they came into their own. The Mid-Suffolk Light Railway played its part when the United States Army Air Forces arrived at the airfields at Mendlesham and Horham. The line had been poorly used before this but was very busy carrying supplies and men to and from the airfields. The war was, however, the peak of the line's existence and it closed shortly after the war. It is now a busy heritage railway and museum.

The Helston Railway, in Cornwall, was part of the GWR. It was mainly used for agricultural purposes although it did see some tourist traffic in the summer. This was another line that has an important wartime connection. Nancegollan became a busy goods base for The Admiralty. After the war, the line became less viable and was closed in the 1960s. It is now a busy heritage railway.

Heritage railways in the UK are mainly run by volunteers and enthusiasts, although some do employ staff. Unfortunately, many of these volunteers are older men and as the railways lose these older volunteers, many of the skills needed to run a steam railway will die out with them. Hopefully, this will not lead to the disappearance of what are not only memories of wartime, but also of the complete history of railways.

Listing all the heritage railway lines is beyond the scope of this book, but each line had its own character. If you want to see steam trains in action, they are the places to visit. A journey on a heritage railway is perhaps the only way to experience what travelling on a wartime railway was like – albeit without the bombs!

104. *Thomas the Tank Engine* on the Watercress Railway. The Mid-Hants Railway became known as the Watercress Line as it used to carry locally produced watercress. It played an important part in the war, facilitating military traffic between the army town of Aldershot and the military embarkation port at Southampton. (*Lucy Colgrove*)

Second World War railway memorials

The number of Second World War railway memorials is much smaller than for the First World War. This is due to the fact that there were fewer railway companies in the last war after the formation of the Big Four. Many Second World War memorials were added to those already in place commemorating railway workers of the First World War.

Abergavenny Town Hall, Monmouth

The memorial consists of a brass plaque mounted on a wooden board and lists sixteen employees of the L&NW Railway Locomotive Department, Abergavenny and sub-stations, who lost their lives in the Great War 1914–18. A separate plaque has been added underneath for two employees who died in the Second World War. The memorial was previously situated in the locomotive sheds at Abergavenny.

Attleborough station, Norfolk

A small rectangular memorial tablet above a door inside the station is dedicated to the American airmen based at Deopham Green during the Second World War. The inscription reads: 'Memorial dedicated to the men of the 452nd Bomb Group (H) who sacrificed their lives in World War II that the ideals of democracy might live.'

Balham station, London Underground

A plaque situated at the top of the escalator from the Northern Line platform commemorates civilians and London Transport staff who were killed at this station during the Blitz. Civilians were sheltering in the station on 14 October 1940 when it was hit by a bomb. The plaque replaces two previous memorials, which are now at the London Transport Museum.

Bethnal Green station, London Underground

The memorial stands in the park next to the station. It commemorates the 173 people who died in an accident on the stairway into the station in March 1943. The accident was reported as a direct bombing hit at the time but was caused by the victims being crushed on the stairway.

Birkenhead Central station, Wirral

A small memorial plaque dedicated to Norman Tunna is situated above a fireplace in the booking hall. Tunna was a shunter on the GWR. During an air raid on Morpeth Dock on 26 September 1940, he extinguished two incendiary bombs in a wagon full of bombs, an act of bravery that saved many lives. He was awarded the George Cross in January 1941. He survived the war and lived until 1970.

Blackpool North station, Lancashire

There are two memorial plaques at Blackpool North station relating to the Second World War. One of them remembers 'all the railwaymen and women of Blackpool who did not count the cost in time of conflict'. Below that is another dedicated to the people who died when a plane crashed on Blackpool Central station on 27 August 1941. It also mentions 'Public Citizens and Rescue Services who did all they could to save lives', as well as 'the brave efforts of PC Thomas Beeston (LMS Railway Police)', who saved a young girl during the incident.

Bounds Green station, London Underground

A memorial plaque is situated on a wall of the westbound platform and is dedicated to 'the sixteen Belgian refugees and the three British citizens who died on this platform during the air raid of 13 October 1940'. The station, which was being used as an air raid shelter, was damaged when a bomb landed on houses above, causing the north end of the westbound tunnel to collapse. Although the plaque was unveiled in 1994, the number and nationality of the casualties has been disputed. Records suggest that sixteen people were killed outright, with a further death the following day, three of which were Belgian refugees.

Brighton station, East Sussex

A bronze memorial plaque that commemorates the fallen railway workers of the First and Second World Wars is situated on a wall at the west side of the station between two arched windows of a shop, which was once the station cafeteria. It was originally unveiled in 1921 to honour the 5,635 members of the staff of the London, Brighton and South Coast Railway Co, who 'joined the forces of the Crown during the war of 1914–1918'. There is a list of names of those who lost their lives in the Great War. The inscription also is dedicated to 'the memory of 626 men of the Southern Railway who gave their lives in the 1939–1945 war', but doesn't list their names.

Christ Church, Crewe, Cheshire

A sandstone memorial situated in the gardens of the church commemorates twenty men from the Crewe tranship shed of the London & North Western Railway who lost their lives in the First World War, with the addition of five names of those lost in the Second World War, when it was part of the LMS. The memorial plaque was moved to its current site in 1999 from its original location in the Basford Hall sidings on Gresty Road.

Crewe station, Cheshire

A brass plaque dedicated to those from the L&NWR Crewe North and South Steam Sheds lists forty-six names of those who lost their lives during the First World War. A green plaque added below lists six employees who lost their lives in the Second World War. The plaque was originally located on platform 12 but is now on a wall in the First Class lounge.

Eastleigh Museum, Hampshire

A bronze plaque, formerly located at the Alstom Railway Engineering Yard Office Building, lists forty-two employees of the locomotive shops and offices, Eastleigh, who lost their lives in the Great War. An additional plaque at the bottom remembers fifteen staff members who were lost in the Second World War, listing their names.

Engine Shed Museum, Severn Valley Railway, Highley, Shropshire

Mounted on the wall of the museum is a large, handwritten roll of honour that gives rank, name, service details and where buried of those who died while serving in Royal Engineers Railway Transportation Units during the Second World War. Included is Lieutenant Colonel Sir Nigel Gresley CBE, who died on 5 April 1941.

Euston station, London

The memorial obelisk that stands outside Euston station was originally paid for by donations from staff of the LNWR to commemorate workmates who fell in the First World War. Later, plaques were added to commemorate those who fell in the Second World War, by which time the LNWR had become part of the LMSR.

Glasgow Central station

The memorial comprises a large pillar situated on the station concourse. It commemorates the railwaymen and women of the Caledonian Railway who gave their lives in the First World War. The names are listed on bronze plaques. A further plaque was added for those who died in the Second World War and subsequent conflicts.

Grosmont station, North Yorks

Grosmont station is at the end of the North Yorkshire Moors heritage railway and is where the mainline begins. A memorial at the station commemorates the railwaymen and women and VE-Day.

Guildford station, Surrey

A white marble memorial plaque is mounted on the wall of the entrance hall with the names of the twenty men 'from all departments at Guildford station' who died in the First World War. A smaller plaque has been added to commemorate 626 men of the Southern Railway who gave their lives in the 1939–1945 war. The numbers demonstrate the considerable part the company played in the war.

King's Cross station, London

The war memorial that now stands at King's Cross station was unveiled in 2013 after the major redevelopment of the site. It comprises eleven marble tablets in individual steel frames listing the 937 employees of the Great Northern Railway who lost their lives in the First World War, with a further dedication to employees of the London and North Eastern Railway who lost their lives in the Second World War. The tablets were part of the original memorial erected in 1920 by the GNR. Those lost in the Second World War are not named.

Letchworth Garden City station, Hertfordshire

Three bronze plaques list 187 men from the area who died in the Second World War, as well as those who died in the Egypt and Suez Crisis of 1951–56. It is situated in Station Place, in a garden behind the First World War memorial.

Liverpool Street station, London

The Kindertransport statue of three children on the forecourt of Liverpool Street station commemorates the 10,000 children who were taken from Germany before the Second World War. The majority of them travelled by rail from Harwich to London.

London Bridge station

Originally unveiled in 1922, a bronze memorial plaque at London Bridge station honours the employees of the London, Brighton and South Coast

Railway who fought in the First and Second World Wars. The top section lists the 5,635 members of staff who 'joined the forces of the Crown during the war of 1914–1918', with five long column lists of those 'who gave their lives for victory in that great struggle to secure the liberty of the world'. Below that is another plaque with the simple dedication to 'The six hundred and twenty-six men of the Southern Railway who gave their lives in the 1939–1945 war'. Their names are not listed.

Lowestoft station, Suffolk

A blue plaque on a wall near the station entrance commemorates 520 children who arrived at the station in 1938 as part of the Kindertransport scheme. The inscription reads: 'In December 1938, Lowestoft Station was the arrival point of a Kindertransport train. The train transported mainly Jewish children as refugees, escaping persecution prior to the outbreak of World War II.'

Maidenhead station, Berkshire

There is a statue of Sir Nicholas Winton sitting on a bench at the station. In 1938, Winton (a Maidenhead resident) went to Czechoslovakia and rescued 669 Jewish refugee children as the Kindertransport scheme only operated in Germany and Austria. He organised eight trains to transport the children from Prague to London and found foster families for them in Britain.

Manchester Piccadilly station

A bronze plaque in a wooden frame with the LMS monogram of the London, Midland and Scottish Railway, commemorates eleven staff who 'served in the world war and made the supreme sacrifice', listing the rank and name of each. It is situated on a wall near the Fairfield Street entrance.

March station, Cambridgeshire

A memorial plaque in the booking hall commemorates engine driver Benjamin Gimbert and his fireman, James Nightall, the heroes who prevented an ammunition train from catching fire on 2 June 1944, and saving the town of Soham from further disaster. The men were awarded the George Cross.

Middlesbrough station, North Yorkshire

There is a small plaque on the wall of the station with the names of those railway personnel and civilians who died in an air raid in August 1942. It is interesting that the plaque is underneath a larger plaque to a British Railway works officer responsible for improving the stations.

Norwich station, Norfolk

A memorial plaque, situated on a wall on the concourse facing the platforms, names the station staff who died in the Second World War at the station. They died on two separate attacks, 9 July and 1 August 1940, and their names are listed.

Paddington station, London

Halfway along platform one at Paddington station is the Great Western Railway War Memorial to the memory of employees of the GWR who died in the First World War. An inscription on the plinth reads: 'In honour of those who served in the world wars 1914 + 1918 1939 + 1945'.

Porthmadog station, Gwynedd

There is a memorial inside Spooner's Bar at Porthmadog Harbour railway station that commemorates No. 2 Dutch Commando, who used the station from August 1942 as their HQ and quarters while training in Wales during the Second World War.

Ramsgate station, Thanet, Kent

A memorial plaque at Ramsgate station commemorates two train drivers – C. Cotton and W. Edwards – as being 'killed by enemy action'. Charles Cotton was killed by a bomb at Deal station and W. Edwards was machine-gunned at Westhanger station.

Retford station, Nottinghamshire

A stone tablet mounted on slate is located on a wall at the south end of the row of buildings on platform 1. The inscription reads: 'The W.V.S. of Retford, March 1940 to March 1946, used these premises as a canteen and rest room. Serving to H.M. and Allied forces 2,284,000 meals during the Second World War.'

Royal Engineers Museum, Brompton Barracks, Chatham, Kent

Two books of remembrance for the Royal Engineers Railway Transportation Unit are kept at the barracks, which is now home to the Royal School of Military Engineering.

Rugby, Warwickshire

A rectangular bronze plaque mounted on a wooden board commemorates sixteen rail workers from Rugby Steam Shed who were lost in the First World War, listing surnames and initials. Below that is a small plaque listing the surnames of twenty who were lost in the Second World War. The memorial was originally located at Rugby station, which closed in 1969, but is now at the plant depot of Colas Rail in Mill Road.

Soham, Cambridgeshire

A Portland stone memorial with a bronze inlay was unveiled in 2007 in Red Lion Square. Artwork on the memorial shows a damaged train and gives details of the incident on 2 June 1944 involving Benjamin Gimbert and James Nightall and how they saved Soham by driving a burning ammunition wagon away from the rest of the train.

A stone tablet inside St Andrew's Church commemorates the 'heroic action of Fireman J.W. Nightall G.C. who gave his life & Driver B. Gimbert G.C. who was badly injured whilst detaching a blazing wagon from an Ammunition train at Soham station at 1.43 a.m. June 2nd 1944. The station was totally destroyed & considerable damage was done by the explosion. The devotion to duty of these brave men saved the town of Soham from grave destruction. Signalman Bridges was killed whilst on duty & Guard H. Clarke suffered from shock.'

Southampton Docks, Hampshire

There are various memorials in the dock. On the North Pier dock, gate 8, is a plaque presented to the Southern Railway by the American army in memory of those who left from the port for Europe. There are also memorials to the LSWR, SR and United Nations Forces in various positions.

A rectangular metal plaque unveiled in 1995 at the Management Office, Town Quay, commemorates the 'men and women of this city whose work in the Southampton Docks and elsewhere made possible the invasion of Europe fifty years ago. Thanks to their efforts, over three and a half million men and women, together with four and a half million tons of cargo, passed through the port between D-Day and the end of the war.'

Southwark, London

On Druid Street, a blue plaque commemorates the incident on 25 October 1940 when a bomb fell through the railway arch, killing seventy-seven people who were sheltering from an air raid.

On Stainer Street, a blue plaque commemorates the people killed and injured when a bomb fell on a railway arch where people were sheltering on 17 February 1941. The plaque states that sixty-eight died and 175 were injured.

St Michael's Church, Lancing, West Sussex

A memorial for men from the Lancing Railway and Carriage Works (then part of the SR) who died in both world wars stands in the grounds of St Michael's church, behind the town's war memorial.

Staplehurst station, Kent

A rectangular brass plaque at the station approach commemorates Pilot Officer Georges Louis Joseph Doutrepont, aged 27, of the Belgian Air Force and 229 Squadron Royal Air Force, 'who lost his life at this spot while flying Hurricane N2537 in combat on ... 15 September 1940', and Southern Railways Booking Clerk Charles Alfred Ashdown, aged 18, 'who lost his life when the Hurricane struck this station'.

Tongham, Surrey

Tongham railway station was demolished after closing in 1960. A brass plaque, erected in 1996 at the junction of The Street and Poyle Road, commemorates George Keen and George Leach, the two Southern Railway men who separated burning trucks from the rest of a train on 22 August 1940 at Tongham station. Both men were awarded the George Cross.

Waterloo station, London

There are various railway memorials in the Victory Arch at the station. These include plaques for both world wars. One mentions the 626 men of the Southern Railway who died in the Second World War. There is also a fiftieth anniversary plaque of D-Day, 6 June 1994, which mentions the railwaymen who died then.

Waverley station, Edinburgh

The large memorial in Waverley station commemorates the men and women of the North British Railway who lost their lives in both world wars. Underneath three large bronze tablets that list all those lost in the First World War is a small plaque with the inscription: 'In memory of all railway men and women who gave their lives in the 1939–45 conflict.' Unlike the Great War memorial above it, it doesn't list their names.

York

The North Eastern Railway War Memorial, situated at the Station Approach, commemorates the employees of the NER who were killed in the First World war. Behind the stone of remembrance are fifteen slates set into the floor of the memorial in 1984, bearing the names of 551 LNER employees who lost their lives in the Second World War.

There are also a number of Second World War memorials in the collection of the National Railway Museum at York, including nameplates of commemorative locomotives.

Commemorative Second World War locomotives and railway vehicles

T here were a number of locomotives and railway vehicles named after men or units involved in conflict. Some locos still exist, whilst others have been broken up but their nameplate still exists. The Battle of Britain class locos were made by the Southern Railway after the war.

Alnwick, Northumberland Fusiliers Museum

LMS Patriot class loco, *Private W. Wood VC* (nameplate) and LMS Patriot class loco, *Private E. Sykes VC* (nameplate).The LNWR named three of their Patriot class locos after surviving VC winners who were employed by them. The other was named after J. Christie. When the old Patriot class locos went out of service, the LMS, who had taken over the LNWR, replaced two of the nameplates on new Patriot class locos. These were named after Wood and Sykes, who were still employed by them.

Bodiam station, East Sussex

The Cavel Van was a prototype parcel and miscellaneous car built by the SE&CR in 1919. It carried the bodies of Edith Cavell and Captain Charles Fryatt, who had both been executed by the Germans, back to Britain after the war. The Cavel Van was restored in 2010 by the Kent and East Sussex Railway.

Bridgenorth, Severn Valley Railway, Shropshire

The Battle of Britain class *Sir Keith Park* locomotive was built in Brighton in 1947. It was named after Air Vice Marshal Park and is now based at the Swanage Railway.

Cottesmore, Rutland Railway Museum

The locomotive *Singapore* was captured at Singapore Naval Dockyard in February 1942. It has memorial plaques to the men who were POWs of the Japanese in Singapore.

Edinburgh

Battle of Britain class loco *603 Squadron* (nameplate and plaque) made a record amount at auction in 1996 for the Edinburgh headquarters of the long-disbanded Royal Auxiliary Air Force Squadron, which is now the base of No. 2 (City of Edinburgh) Maritime Headquarters Unit. The 603 City of Edinburgh Squadron was a fighter unit involved in the Battle of Britain and was one of the SR Battle of Britain class named locomotives.

Highley, Engine House, Severn Valley Railway, Shropshire

Royal Engineers Military Railway Unit loco 8233 (later 48773). The Locomotive was built in 1940 by the Northern British Locomotive Company for the War Department for use in France. As France had fallen by this time it was leant to the LMS. In 1941, it was sent to Persia to help supply the Russians.

Manston Museum, Kent

SR Battle of Britain class loco *222 Squadron* (nameplate). There were forty-four Battle of Britain Class locos built for the SR. The squadron was active at Dunkirk and in the Battle of Britain. It later became the first jet fighter unit of the RAF.

March Museum, Cambridgeshire

Two class 47 locomotive nameplates named after Benjamin Gimbert GC and James Nightall GC, the heroes of Soham.

Mangapps Railway Museum, Burnham-on-Crouch, Essex

In 1981 a class 47 locomotive was named *James Nightall GC*. The nameplate was removed in 1995. The locomotive was preserved at the museum and new nameplates were fitted.

Cosford RAF Museum, Shifnal, Shropshire

SR Battle of Britain class loco *615 Squadron* (nameplate and plaque). The squadron was named County of Surrey and played a part in the Battle of Britain before moving to Burma.

Cosford RAF Museum Reserve Collection, Shifnal, Staffordshire

SR Battle of Britain class loco *Croydon* (nameplate).
229 Squadron (nameplate and plaque).
249 Squadron (nameplate and plaque).
46 Squadron (nameplate and plaque).
264 Squadron (nameplate and plaque).
141 Squadron (plaque).
253 Squadron (nameplate and plaque).
501 Squadron (nameplate and plaque).
219 Squadron (nameplate).
602 Squadron (nameplate).
Sir Trafford Leigh Mallory (nameplate).
Sir Keith Park (nameplate).
Royal Observer Corps (nameplate).
Fighter Command (nameplate).
Hurricane (nameplate).
Spitfire (nameplate).

Sheffield, Royal Victoria Holiday Inn, South Yorkshire

Valour railway loco 66175 (duplicate nameplate), with an inscription: 'Valour. In memory of all railway employees who gave their lives for their country.'

Sheffield Park Station, Bluebell Railway, East Sussex

SR Battle of Britain class loco *Sir Archibald Sinclair*. Sinclair was a Liberal MP who became Secretary of State for Air during the war.

Norbury School, Hazel Grove, Stockport, Greater Manchester

LMS Patriot class loco 5536 *Private W. Wood VC* (nameplate). In 1922, an LNWR Claughton locomotive was named after Wood, who was one of their employees.

Swanage Railway, Dorset

SR Battle of Britain class loco *Manston*, named after the Second World War airfield in Kent.

Swanage, Herston Works, Dorset

SR Battle of Britain class loco *257 Squadron*. The squadron was mainly based in the South East early in the war and became one of the first units to be given Hawker Typhooons.

Nene Valley Railway, Wansford, Cambridgeshire

SR Battle of Britain class loco *92 Squadron*. The squadron was the first to receive Spitfires in 1940.

York, National Railway Museum

LNWR Prince of Wales class loco 2275 *Edith Cavell* (nameplate).
LBSCR Remembrance class locos (nameplates 1 & 2).
SR Battle of Britain class loco *Winston Churchill*.
SR Battle of Britain class loco *605 Squadron* (plaque).
SR Battle of Britain class loco *Sir Trafford Leigh Mallory* (nameplate).

Mobile locos

GWR Hitachi IEP train 800306, named after both Lance Corporal Allen Leonard Lewis VC and Flight Sub Lieutenant Harold Day DSC, and the fallen of the GWR.

LNER Electric class 91 111 loco, named *For the Fallen* in 2014 at Newcastle Station.

LNER Electric class 91 110 loco, *Battle of Britain*.

GWR, Didcot Parkway station, High Speed Railway Power car No. 43087 11, Explosive Ordnance Disposal Regiment Royal Logistics Corps.

DB Cargo UK class 66 loco 66077 *Benjamin Gimbert GC*.

GB Rail freight class 66 loco 66715, *Valour Railway*.

SET Unit 465 903 *Remembrance*.

DB Cargo UK class 66 loco 66 100, *Armistice 100*.

Southall SR Battle of Britain class loco *Tangmere*. Tangmere was a Second World War airfield near Chichester.

Glossary

ARP	Air Raid Precautions
ASLEF	Associated Society of Locomotive Steam Enginemen and Firemen
BEF	British Expeditionary Force
BNCR	Belfast and Northern Counties Railway
DSC	Distinguished Service Cross
ECML	East Coast Main Line
GC	George Cross
GNR	Great Northern Railway
GWR	Great Western Railway
LMS	London, Midland and Scottish Railway
L&NWR	London and North Western Railway
LNER	London and North Eastern Railway
LPTB	London Passenger Transport Board
MoWT	Ministry of War Transport
NUR	National Union of Railwaymen
RCA	Railway Clerks' Association of Great Britain & Ireland
RE	Royal Engineers
SE&CR	South Eastern & Chatham Railway
SR	Southern Railway
UERL	Underground Electric Railways Company of London Limited
VC	Victoria Cross

Bibliography

Books

Bell, W.J., *Recent Locomotives of the London Midland & Scottish Railway*, Virtue, 1940

British Railways in Peace and War, British Railways Press Office, 1944

Bryan, T., *All in a Day's Work: Life on the GWR*, Ian Allen, 2004

Calder, A., *The People's War: Britain 1939–1945*, Jonathon Cape, 1969

Darwin, B., *War on the Line*, Southern Railway Co., 1946

Hind, J.R., *The British Railways Can Take It*, Valentine & Sons, 1944

Hungerford, E., *Transport for War 1942–1943*, E.P. Dutton & Co., 1943

It Can Now be Revealed: More about British Railways in Peace and War, British Railways Press Office, 1945

Jenkins, T., *Sir Ernest Lemon: A Biography*, Railway and Canal Historical Society, 2011

John, E., *Timetable for Victory*, British Railways, 1946

Kalla-Bishop, P.M., *Locomotives at War: Army Railway Reminiscences of the Second War*, Bradford Barton, 1980

Kay, P., *The Corringham Light Railway: A New History*, Peter Kay, 2008

Ludlam, A.J., *The RAF Cranwell Railway*, Oakwood, 1988

Major, S., *Female Railway Workers in World War II*, Pen & Sword, 2018

Nash, G.C., *The LMS at War*, London, Midland & Scottish Railway, 1946

National Service, His Majesty's Stationary Office, 1939

Oldham, K., *Steam in Wartime Britain*, Sutton, 1993

Seaborne, M., *Shelters: Living Underground in the London Blitz*, Nishen Photography, 1988

Sullivan, Maj W.W., *Accomplishments of the Military Railways*, Railway Accounting Officers Association, 1919

The Locomotives of the Southern Railway (Western Section), W.G. Tilling, 1943

Turley, A., *The Railway at Kidderminster in the 1940s*, Adrian & Neil Turley, 2005

Whitehouse, P. & Thomas, D. St John, *The Great Western Railway: 150 Glorious Years*, David & Charles, 1984

Wildish, G.N., *Engines of War*, Ian Allen, 1946

Zaloga, S.J., *Railway Guns of World War II*, Osprey, 2016

Newspapers & periodicals

Hampshire Chronicle: 27 September 1856

Kidderminster Shuttle: 3 July 1943

Manchester Guardian: 28 December 1940, 16 January 1941, 13 April 1941, 28 November 1942, 8 July 1943, 18 January 1944, 2 June 1944

Railway Magazine: October 1931, December 1931, April 1935, May 1935, November 1937, February 1940, March 1940, July 1941, November 1941, January 1947, February 1947

The Times: 5 November 1940, 5 November 1941, 4 November 1942, 6 July 1943, 17 January 1944, 7 February 1944, 19 February 1944, 6 January 1945, 3 March 1945

National Archive documents

CAB 565/9/11, War Cabinet

CAB 65/9/27, War Cabinet

CAB 65/9/36, War Cabinet

Cab 66/11/48, Effects of Air Raids on Railways

Cab 66/17/46, Control and Higher Organisation of the Railways

CAB 67/8/28

CAB 67/8/70, Financial Arrangements for Railway

CAB 67/8/75, Air Raid Shelter Policy

CAB 79/8/60, Long Range Artillery

FO 371/32221/16, Trading with the Enemy

MEPO 4/490

Index

Air raid shelters, 23, 55–6, 72–4, 77–9, 84–5, 94–5, 120–1

Big Four, 6–15, 21–3, 34, 37–8, 43, 47, 51, 58–9, 68, 84, 103–104, 106, 136, 141–2, 161, 172, 179,189–90, 198
Birmingham, 30, 69, 90, 95, 109, 117, 123, 167, 194
Bombing, 28, 31, 34, 39, 45, 60–1, 65, 67–9, 71–4, 77, 80–6, 88, 94–5, 97–9, 102–106, 113, 116–17, 121–3, 127, 131–4, 136, 142–3, 145–7, 150, 156–7, 169–70, 177–9, 180, 196, 199
British Rail, 23, 34, 37, 47, 51, 68, 130, 136, 141–2, 148, 189, 194, 196, 204

D-Day, 58, 73, 105, 142–3, 155, 159, 165–6, 168, 172–4, 176–8, 184, 188, 206–207
Docks, 5, 7, 13–14, 21, 23, 26, 33, 39–40, 45–50, 55, 57–9, 69, 71–2, 75, 99, 128, 140–4, 152, 159, 173, 184, 190, 199, 206, 209
Dover, 39, 46, 58–61, 66–7, 69, 70–3, 131, 178, 188
Dunkirk, 48, 57–9, 63–9, 106, 117, 130, 143, 209

Evacuation, 25, 28, 30–3, 35–6, 38, 46, 59, 61, 65, 69, 75, 85, 102, 106, 108

Glasgow, 13, 30, 51, 72, 92, 105, 116, 118, 123, 140, 151, 158, 173, 201
Great Western Railway, 1, 6–7, 9, 10, 13, 15–17, 22, 42, 48–9, 51–4, 58–9, 60–1, 64–5, 70, 72, 75, 86–8, 92–3, 95, 98, 104–108, 123, 127–8, 138, 142, 144, 152, 155–6, 165, 176, 180, 187, 190, 196–7, 199, 204, 212

Liverpool, 9, 13, 21, 28, 30, 46, 59, 81–3, 99, 105–106, 109, 113, 116, 173, 175
London, 8–10, 12–13, 16–17, 21–2, 28, 31–6, 41, 45, 47, 49, 51–2, 60, 63–4, 66, 68, 73–4, 76–80, 82–3, 85–6, 90, 95–7, 104, 106, 108–109, 111–12, 120, 122, 126, 129, 134, 142, 144, 148–9, 152, 163, 168–9, 175–9, 163, 186, 191, 195, 201–204, 206–207
London, Midland and Scottish Railway, 7, 27, 57, 59, 62, 107, 201, 203
London and North Eastern Railway, 6, 8–9, 15–16, 22–3, 39, 48–9, 59, 64, 75, 80, 83, 86, 91–3, 95–6, 105, 107, 116, 122–3, 128–9, 131, 137, 142, 144, 146–7, 150, 153–4, 161–2, 168–9, 174, 179, 180, 184–7, 193, 202, 207, 212
London Passenger Transport Board, 6, 12–13, 23, 30, 132
London Underground, 12–13, 18, 21, 28, 50, 56, 72, 74, 77, 81, 84, 90, 95, 97, 144, 148, 198–9

Manchester, 9, 23, 28, 30, 35, 50, 53, 61–2, 82, 85–6, 89, 99, 109, 116, 140, 149, 150, 153, 156, 175, 178, 183–4, 195, 203, 211
Metropolitan Line, 12, 90, 180

Railway Executive Committee, 5, 7, 14, 20–4, 34, 36, 48, 57–8, 82, 89, 108, 110, 131–2, 136, 168

Royal Engineers, 2–5, 54–5, 77, 92, 177, 196, 201, 205, 209

Sheffield, 9, 17, 30, 50, 120, 154, 175, 179, 210, 211
Ships, 14, 48–9, 58–9, 64–5, 75, 92, 99, 128, 130, 142–3, 168, 173
Southampton, 39, 40, 47, 57–8, 60–1, 72, 76, 86, 106, 160, 165, 173, 184, 197, 206
Southern Railway, 6–7, 10, 15, 22, 36, 39–40, 43–5, 47, 58–60, 67–8, 75, 83, 86, 94, 102, 105, 129, 142, 147, 149–50, 154, 161, 171–2, 177, 181, 184, 200, 202–203, 206–208, 209–12
Swindon, 9, 104, 108, 115, 127, 133, 137, 185, 190

Women, 25, 28, 53, 59, 94, 98–101, 104, 110, 112, 116–17, 121, 125–6, 128, 132–3, 139, 146–9, 151, 158, 165, 167, 169, 179, 187, 189–92, 199, 201, 206, 207

York, 16, 49, 122, 124, 131, 133, 207, 211